"With this book Carole brings the magic of brain scienc
teamwork and projects using examples from real project professionals and
explanations from some of the foremost brain, behavioral and social scientists ...

This book takes the project professional deeper into the science and practice
of brain science on projects ... to create a framework of practices and behaviours
that will help any project team perform to a higher level and experience higher
levels of wellbeing."

Ruth Pearce, the Project Manager Burnout Coach, member of the Advisory Board
of the Institute for Neuro & Behavioral Project Management and author of *Be a
Project Motivator*

"What makes the difference between success and failure is always 'the people
stuff'. Most of us don't understand why people behave as they do as individuals
and, crucially, as teams. We know that stressful environments and experiences
lead to poor delivery and poor mental health ... Carole provides actionable advice,
skills, tools and case studies for practical, mindful results."

Keith Leslie, Chair of Samaritans in UK & Ireland and author of *A Question Of
Leadership*

"There are two facts every project and programme manager should know:
1) managing change is complex; 2) the human brain is the most complex entity in
the known universe.

Unfortunately, few people seem to connect these facts - and then they wonder
why their change projects fail.

This book explains how to practically manage the complexities of human
behaviour in a project environment. Read it and deliver!"

Stephen Carver, Speaker in Change and Crisis Management at Cranfield
University School of Management

Neuroscience for project success

Contents

Contents

Part 3: Tools to improve delivery performance

Contents

Part 4. Integrating neuroscience into your projects

List of figures

Foreword

We need to reduce the number of projects that fail, in every sector.

We have the methods, tools and techniques in project, programme and change management to manage the processes needed to deliver change. However, we often fail to: 1) engage stakeholders effectively, 2) model appropriate behaviours, and 3) put sufficient focus on embedding changes so they become the new normal. The net result is that we don't achieve the intended outcomes and benefits.

An understanding of neuroscience and how the brain works can provide insights into why projects fail, and in what ways emotions and behaviours have an impact. Understanding (and learning to recognise) your own and others' emotional responses can help with engaging stakeholders, risk assessment and decision making, and improving leadership and teams.

Specifically targeted at project professionals in all sectors and all types of projects, programmes and PMOs, this book is a significant step forward because it focuses on a critical missing link of change delivery – the human factor.

Even now project management education focuses over 90 per cent of its curriculum on the processes for designing, planning and coordinating the delivery of projects, and yet the most difficult elements to navigate are the sponsors, stakeholders and end users, because they are driven by emotions that don't fit into the logical case for change.

If we are to genuinely deliver sustainable benefits for society and improve products and services that meet the needs of the populations we serve, then we as project and change professionals need the knowledge and skills to navigate the emotional mindsets of the people we are working with and for.

Neuroscience for project success brings together an understanding of neuroscience with tools and techniques to enable project and change professionals to build their own, and their team's, emotional resilience, and to engage others to successfully deliver sustainable change. We just need to apply it!

Jo Stanford ChPP,
Head of Project Profession, Health Education England,
November 2021

Part 1. Setting the scene

1

Introduction

Imagine asking a doctor to be a doctor without a grasp of physiology, or a linguist to produce a translation without any knowledge of grammar. Yet we've been asking people to deliver huge projects, with big people-impacts, for years. And we haven't given them a model that clearly explains 'why people behave the way they do'. It's crazy!

Does it matter? Yes, it does – because many in the project world find the people stuff so difficult to get their heads around.

I'm not being critical; it's not surprising. A robust model to explain why people behave as they do did not exist. But that's no longer the case. Advances in neuroscience[i] have filled that gap – we have a model. And, as we'll see in this book, its existence offers new and helpful ways to think about the challenges of project and programme delivery – no matter how big or small your project is, what it aims to achieve, or what industry you are in.

In the same way, it doesn't matter if you're just starting out or you've been in the profession for years. The ideas presented here are relevant whether you're grappling with uncertainty, stress and the complexity of human behaviour; your focus is on accurately weighing risks and making good decisions; or you want to prove yourself as a project professional.

I'm not exaggerating when I say the material here has the potential to turn the world on its head – in a good way, because it will enable you to understand, possibly for the first time, why people behave as they do.

I don't want you to take my word for it. Read on, make notes, and come to your own conclusions.

The book is organised as follows:

Part 1: Setting the scene, includes this introduction. Chapter 2, Projects today offers tales from the dark side and practitioners' perspectives.

Part 2: You, your projects and your brain begins with Chapter 3, Why people behave as they do. This includes brain basics, an introduction to emotions and social threat and a framework for understanding whether our Thinking brain is online or offline. These themes are developed in Chapter 4, Groups and stress

---

[i] The science of the brain and the nervous system

make VUCA (volatile, uncertain, complex, and ambiguous) more VUCA, as I weave them with insights into how to create a psychologically safe or, if you get it wrong, a toxic project culture. Chapter 5, Skills that everybody needs, builds on these lessons to redefine emotional intelligence, explore memory, and illustrate how and why we need to be more mindful and cognitively ready – for mental health and decision making. Chapter 6, The way we see the world, adds new dimensions to your understanding of the human brain and prompts you to reflect on whether the perspectives you bring to your projects help or hinder delivery.

Part 3: Tools to improve delivery performance is primarily a toolkit. Chapter 7, Start by looking in on yourself, introduces the idea that we all contribute to the situations we find ourselves in. It provides tools to help you reflect on your attitude to risk and uncertainty; the stories that you tell; and your emotions and behaviours. The tools, marked with a spanner icon, are designed to inspire you to experiment with different approaches and they are supported by stories from project professionals who have done just that. Chapter 8, Looking outside yourself, expands the frame to take in team members and stakeholders, and to explore how the frameworks introduced in Chapters 3-7 can be used to keep other people's Thinking brains online. It goes on to offer tools that pick up the remaining themes identified by practitioners in Part 1, vision and embedding change.

Part 4: Integrating neuroscience into your projects, starts with four case studies in Chapter 9. Each one offers a deep dive into a project from a different sector and illustrates how the programme lead has used lessons from the earlier chapters. Chapter 10, Overturning command and control, builds on the case studies and consolidates the themes and learning.

You may be on a development journey that is aligned to the requirements of a professional body such as the Association for Project Management (APM), Project Management Institute (PMI) or the Change Management Institute (CMI). If you are wondering, 'how do the ideas in this book support my professional development?' or 'how do I use them to best effect?' you'll find high-level answers in Appendix A and Appendix B.

Outcomes for you

You will go away with:

- a robust model that you can return to, again and again, to address the people challenges on your projects and programmes;

- new insights into:
  - yourself, and what drives your struggles, decisions, emotions and actions;
  - the behaviour of stakeholders, customers, and team members;
  - the additional dynamics that arise in groups and systems;
- new perspectives on the causes of stress and complexity, and techniques for reducing both;
- tools and frameworks to apply and experiment with.

Jo Stanford set out the challenges to the profession in the Foreword. My aim in writing this book is to give you the skills, confidence and ability to meet them head-on.

2

Projects today

When I started writing this book I promised myself that it would be grounded in reality – the reality of practising project professionals. Behind the scenes of every story of succeeding against the odds, there are other stories that rarely get airtime.

This chapter starts with some snapshots from the dark side, as a reminder of the many aspects of project life that often get glossed over in the literature. It goes on to ask how we might understand the bigger picture that's driving them.

In answering this question, we need to recognise that the picture we see depends on where we are standing. The second half of this chapter provides an opportunity to stand in different places and compare perspectives about the challenges of delivery.

Snapshots from the dark side

I'm not going to divulge my sources, but I want you to know I have not made any of these snapshots up.

- *I used to be the subject matter expert running a team inside my organisation. Now, most of my team members are based in different organisations. Some specialise in disciplines I hadn't heard of three years ago! How can I hold them to account and do my job, when half the time I don't really understand what they're talking about?* **Project manager**
- *Don't get me started on stakeholders. I got used to stakeholder management, and I was OK at it. But now they tell me I must engage with stakeholders – not like the captain of a galleon engages with the enemy, but to get them engaged. What's that all about?* **Project manager**
- *Six months after joining the project, I came out of yet another meeting thinking, 'I knew it would be difficult, but not this difficult'. With a sinking stomach I turned to my deputy and asked, 'How many more stones have we got to look under only to find something really nasty?'. 'Oh' he replied, 'we're about halfway through'.* **Programme director**

- *The programme manager reports progress with a standard slide deck. What they say is not quite believable, but it's very slick, and somehow, they carry it off. All of us are uncomfortable with this ritual, yet nobody quite knows quite how interrupt them ... We need good governance, not this!* **Programme director**
- *When you don't know, the worst thing you can do is to pretend that you do know. The trouble for many of us is, that throughout our careers we have been encouraged, in very subtle ways, to pretend the opposite – that we do know, when we don't.* **Programme manager**
- *It's relentless, and the volume and the pace of change is not going to slow down. Many people are just overwhelmed.*
  In the past we could say, 'The emotional side is difficult, but there will be time to process it.' We knew that once the tangible changes from the project management side, and the new processes, standards and policies from the change side were in place, we'd reach a plateau. There'd be time to exhale and say, 'Thank God for that' and take time to bed things down.
  Bedding down, through repeating new ways of doing things, is crucial. It moves you from the 'I've kind of grasped it' to being able to do it without really thinking.
  These days, the bedding down rarely happens. We get to 'I've just about grasped it', and we are slammed from the other side with another change. It might be because of changes by our suppliers to third party systems, or new regulatory demands. Typically, we have limited influence and are simply plunged into the next level of uncertainty. We never get a chance to go, 'I've had a great morning. I've completed something. I've done that task well – I am competent.' **Change manager**
- *I've been in many situations where people take false comfort in detail to feel better about uncertainty. They'll say: 'There's a 70-page report so it must be right', followed by 'Yes, and our assurance people have written 78 pages on why it's a good report, so we've got two lines of defence'.*
  The whole reporting thing becomes an exercise in justifying, rather than assessing 'are we generally doing the right thing?'. And it's easier to write 70 pages that don't say anything, than two crunchy ones. **PMO lead**
- *When you're overloaded and so much is moving that you are unable to pin down all the interdependencies, it's really hard to make good decisions. As a result, the board will often avoid decisions on priorities and you get one change piled on top of another, on top of another. It becomes a game. One chief executive I worked with compared it to Buckaroo. Do you remember*

that kids' game with a plastic mule? At the start the mule stands on all four feet and has a blanket on its back. You take turns piling things onto it. If you're clumsy, or add one thing too many, the mule bucks on its front legs and throws everything off. The chief executive knew what he was doing – he told me so. But he couldn't see an alternative. **Consultant**

As we read these snapshots, it's important to remember that we've got a project management focus and there's another side to every one of them! What's more, the picture varies depending on where you stand.

The next section explores how the picture changes according to your role. It is based on interviews with authors and expert practitioners in the disciplines below:

- Project management;
- Programme management;
- Risk management;
- Sponsor or SRO;
- PMO;
- Change management.

Each interview focused on the same question. When it comes to delivery, what are the top two or three challenges people in this discipline repeatedly encounter?

You've probably spotted that I've limited myself to interviewing project and change management professionals. You might want to ask some of *your* key stakeholders about their top challenges – your Head of Finance, Head of IT or Head of PMO may have a very different take on the world. The same goes for external stakeholders.

Practitioners speak about the challenges of delivery

As you read these perspectives, you may find yourself nodding in agreement with what's written, irritated by it, or disagreeing vehemently. Whatever your reaction, it's useful information. If you have a strong reaction, you may want to take a moment to note it down (so you can come back to it once you've learned to decipher your responses), before you continue reading.

A project manager's perspective

For Gordon MacKay, author of *Evolving Project Leadership* and project management capability lead at Sellafield, we can't get away from the fact that the context in which we work has changed massively, and it has changed our understanding of what good project management looks like. With this he sees four challenges:

- shedding the legacy of command and control;
- adopting a new style of (facilitative) leadership;
- being the outsider;
- building a vision as the bridge to collaboration.

Shedding the legacy of command and control

The organisation structures and the environment we're working in have changed, and the role of the project manager has changed too.

As a profession, we've underestimated the extent to which the world would become more volatile, uncertain, complex and ambiguous (VUCA) and the extent we'd be impacted by political, economic, social, technical, legal and environmental change.

There are many project managers with five, 10 or more years of experience, who've been taught that command and control is the way to deliver – and it does not work; in fact it is actively counter-productive and does more harm than good.

Team members who seem uncooperative are often unimpressed by attempts at command and control. I've even seen many of the younger ones greet it looking askance, with a roll of the eyes, and a 'what the hell!'.

It's not surprising so many established project managers find this lack of authority really difficult. It's not their fault. They've been conditioned to deliver in an out-dated, overly assertive way. They've been taught that being a project manager means aggressively holding people to account and dismissing anything else as 'soft'.

It's incredibly challenging for them to shed this legacy of expectations about what good project management looks like. Yet shed it they must, because command and control does not earn respect and is not suited to working in a VUCA world.

What's needed now is leadership – not in the traditional, heroic way, but in the facilitative sense.

Adopting a new style of (facilitative) leadership

Facilitative leadership is not about *me* and what *I need* to get the job done.

It's about recognising our interdependence and what we need from each other to get the job done. It's about knowing that if you get egg on your face, I'll get it on mine too, and vice versa.

It's about developing a vision; realising the potential of each individual and the potential of the team working together, in collaboration, for synergy.

It requires us to be aware of how we are behaving and our impact. Take decision-making, for example. It's one thing to go around the table and ask, 'What do you think? And you? And you? ... This is my decision.'

It's quite another to go around the table asking, 'What do you think?', before moving on to, 'How can we pull this together?' and, 'What's the common ground we can build on?' – eliciting the way forward from the group.

Many project managers find the idea of working like this threatening and disconcerting. Yet they must get past this knee-jerk, emotional response to build skills they need to succeed.

These skills include the self-awareness and self-management of emotional intelligence. The ability to discern what triggers us to behave in unhelpful ways. And, when we do get triggered (as will inevitably happen), the skills to recover quickly and resume working collaboratively.

These in turn will help with the third challenge – the team see you as an outsider.

Being the outsider

It doesn't matter whether you are called a project manager or a project leader, as soon as you step into the role, you are cast as an outsider.

You rapidly become aware that they are the team – they are all with each other, while you are coming in from outside. It doesn't matter if you are joining an existing team, or a team that hasn't worked together before. That sense of 'we' the team, and you the disruptive outsider, is always there at the outset.

The challenge is to work out how you can effectively and competently become accepted. What will it take to be seen as a non-threatening person, on whom they willingly *bestow* the title of 'leader'?

When they bestow that title on you, they are essentially saying, 'I respect you, I'm inspired by you. You see and respect where I'm coming from, I trust you, and I'll go the extra mile for you'.

Getting to this point hinges on your ability to establish rapport with the team and your ability to create a bridge to collaboration.

Building a vision as the bridge to collaboration

For Gordon, this bridge is based on building a shared vision. He emphasises that vision isn't an airy-fairy thing, like a mission statement, that's worked on and never gets read again. The *act* of creating the vision is as important as the content.

The way you create it allows you to make a powerful connection: rapport with the team members. Get it right and you demonstrate reciprocity: 'I respect you. I can learn from you. I see where you're coming from, I trust you and I'll go the extra mile for you'. In other words, all those things you want them to say about you.

A programme manager's perspective

When I spoke with Ruth Murray-Webster, author of *Managing Successful Programmes 5th edition,* about the challenges faced by programme managers, she highlighted:

- Sustaining the vision
- Embedding change
- Governance and assurance

Sustaining the vision

I was interested to see that Ruth also spoke about vision. But she emphasised that when it comes to programme management, the vision challenge has a slightly different flavour. It's about sustaining the vision over time, rather than building a vision as a bridge to collaboration.

According to Ruth, early in the life cycle, building the vision is relatively easy. The programme is new; people are willing to explore the narrative and vision.

However, when you are running a long and complex programme, holding on to that vision is a very different thing. Many programme leads underestimate the energy required to keep the vision focused, refreshed and relevant.

When things change massively, some are slow to realise that the vision needs to pivot and change too. Sometimes though, there are no significant changes that put the vision back onto the radar. When this is the case, remembering to focus on the vision and use it as a key point of reference over time, is very demanding – especially when so much other programme-related stuff is calling you to do big scary things.

The notion of sustaining focus brought Ruth to the second key challenge for programme managers: embedding change.

Embedding change

She points out that most programmes underestimate the amount of really hard work that is needed to get the recipients of change to *actually change* their way of working. We tend to lose sight of the fact that we will be unable to realise the benefits we are seeking, until we have embedded these new capabilities.

Rather than taking responsibility for embedding the changes, there is a tendency to fall back on a narrative of resistance to change; 'We've done everything we can do, but it's difficult to embed the changes because *they* are so resistant to it.'

She sees this as completely misplaced. Her doctorate explored change from the perspective of the *recipients* of change.

Her research included a big university change programme that involved librarians. This quote from one of the librarians illustrates where the project profession goes wrong.

"I know that what you're trying to get us to do is absolutely the right thing. But as a professionally-trained librarian I just can't bring myself to do it."

Think back to a time when you had an 'I just can't bring myself to do it' moment. Now imagine someone describing you as resistant. Would that make you want to co-operate? I'm guessing not! What could they say that might ease the situation just a little?

As soon as we talk about resistance to change, we focus on task and process (what we want people to do and not to do), and we minimise what they think and feel about our changes. As we do this, we get in our own way. We undermine our attempts to embed change.

13

The challenge is to recognise that people's thoughts and feelings about what you are trying to do, are as legitimate as the new ways of working you want to introduce. You need to address both if you are to succeed in embedding your changes.

Ruth identified a third key challenge for programme leads: getting the governance and assurance right.

Governance and assurance

She observes: "I've worked with, and for, lots of programme leads who are not equipped to focus governance conversations. Meetings follow the same pattern and have a set-piece quality.

"I see it most often in organisations where a very seasoned consultant is employed as the programme manager. Reporting progress can become a lie very quickly. Nobody knows how to call it out by asking a question that just cuts through it all, or how to say, 'I really want to talk about this'.

"I put it down to a dissonance between what the organisation investing in the change wants and needs, and what the programme manager and team want and need.

"The programme manager clearly wants and needs to get through the meeting as quickly as possible so they can get back to the doing. Or, if they're going for a decision, they want the answer as quickly as possible so they can get on with implementation.

"If the governance board is going to get to the right decision, they need space to evaluate, 'Is this still the right thing? Is there stuff we need to know now, which will reassure us that we can manage with this? What will give us this reassurance?'

"Many programme leads know that something is not quite right but they struggle to put a finger on what could change."

On the face of it, governance and assurance present a completely different challenge to dealing with resistance to change. But look more closely and you can see there are similarities – both are about having the right conversations.

A risk manager's perspective

Ruth is also an expert in risk management and author of *Understanding and Managing Risk Attitude*, so I took the opportunity to explore the biggest challenges faced by risk managers too. In her view having the conversations you need to have comes top of the list.

Having the conversations you need to have

"Look at the history and you'll see the 'R' word, risk, associated with health and safety and financial risk. Many of those who are responsible for it see their role in terms of convincing the board that the internal controls are working well; after all, we're not bribing anyone, we're not corrupt, and the accounts are OK ... in other words it's all about process.

"This might have worked in the past, but it doesn't now. These days it's not enough to be defensive and focus risk conversations exclusively on protecting value. You must also consider the strategy, the business, and decision making under conditions of uncertainty. Discussing risk helps to create value.

"The project and programme world is getting better at acknowledging uncertainty, but needs to move from saying, 'risk management is difficult and a bit of a waste of time, so you just follow a process', to a point where there are more meaningful conversations to inform decision making.

"These conversations need to include the obvious, 'What do we know and what don't we know?' 'How much is too much?' And so on.

"And they need to go further. During the pandemic, Professor Sir David Spiegelhalter, of Cambridge University, constantly reminded us that 'to understand the numbers, one has to have that critical ability of also examining one's feelings and motivations'.

"When taking risky and important decisions we need to know how we've come to a particular point of view.

"Feelings and motivations are part of the story. You can't get away from them by ignoring them. They inform our view of the future, and they are intensely personal. We must make them explicit if we don't want them to get in the way.

"These conversations are scary!

"Imagine a junior risk analyst trying to have a conversation with a senior leader. They want them to be open about their intentions, motivations and feelings. But it's hard. It's far easier to focus on the numbers and avoid these subjects.

"It happens, even when you've got years of experience. I've been there lots of times, I know there's a different conversation to be had, and I've not dared start it."

Ruth speaks about the challenges of exploring risks with senior leaders. When it comes to project and programme delivery, what are the biggest challenges from their perspective?

A sponsor or SRO's perspective

To answer this question, I spoke to Alistair Godbold, who sat on the APM Board, and Fiona Spencer at the UK Government's Infrastructure and Projects Authority. Before answering, Fiona took a moment to clarify terminology: government projects have a designated senior responsible officer (SRO)[1] rather than a sponsor. The SRO owns the business case and is accountable for successful project delivery. They are the single point of accountability for the project, so the same considerations apply.

Both offered thoughts related to the project life cycle:

- Balancing ambition with reality during the initiation phase.
- Mental gymnastics and holding to the outcomes during the delivery phase.

Balancing ambition with reality during the initiation phase

Major projects typically get started in a blaze of glory, excitement, and ambition for something to happen. People pop up from all over the place and add their two pence about the right way forward. The challenge is to hold off the rush to a solution and make space for quality thinking and planning.

As the sponsor, or SRO, you've got to hang on to your hat and stick to clarifying, 'What's the problem we are trying to solve? What outcomes do we want to achieve? What will success look like in that context? What are the options to get there?'

Slowing down to do this properly and make sure that it's all been encapsulated in the business case is incredibly challenging. The work needs to go beyond a vague statement of vision; it needs to be grounded and layered so there's enough granularity for all your different audiences to understand the outcomes and benefits – what you want to have happened as a result.

In addition, for some megaprojects this stage can take years, and because the big money hasn't been committed, you're often scrabbling around for people to do it. But don't be misled; for a sponsor or SRO, resourcing and finding the right people often remains a challenge throughout the project life cycle – whether it's a megaproject or not.

Like everything in delivery and implementation, resource requirements evolve over time. But it's not enough to sit back and say: 'we'll pick these skills up in the market when we need them'. More than one project has foundered because, when recruitment time comes around, everyone in the market is looking to adopt the same new delivery practices and there simply aren't enough people in the global market with those skills yet. This illustrates the next key challenge – the ability to perform mental gymnastics.

Mental gymnastics and holding to the outcomes during the delivery phase

Sponsors and SROs need a sense of the whole project in their heads, including how to deliver it in real life. They need to take this big, complex picture and translate it, through storytelling, for example, into digestible chunks for their different audiences. And they need to stay grounded and realistic, without ignoring or minimising the uncertainties, throughout.

This is like performing mental gymnastics. It means thinking in 3D, in terms of now and the future, and what's happening on the way to get there, in all its different dimensions, whether that's stakeholders or resources or money.

Holding that evolving picture in your head, and thinking things through, while always trying to think ahead, is a huge challenge.

It's not just a top-down process with you saying, 'this is what I need'; it's also bottom-up. You have to be willing to listen as people come to you saying, 'you've asked me to do this – I've encountered this opportunity or issue'. You need to stay flexible and to control the changes by keeping the outcomes in mind. Sometimes it means saying 'yep, that's a great opportunity, but even so, we're not going to do it'. Or 'we'll consider it later'. Other times, you might agree to pursue it.

The same mental gymnastics are required with delivery partners and stakeholders. On projects, that famous quotation, 'no plan survives first contact with the enemy', is apt. Life happens, and you need to keep the picture in your head relevant and updated.

To do this well, you must be able to manage your emotions, so you can press the pause button to consider, 'What does this mean in terms of my role? How do I, or don't I, intervene?'

A PMO perspective

Katie Hickman of The Nichols Group joined Alistair Godbold to talk about the key challenges for PMO leads. They concluded that in these roles you can't get away from the fact that all projects have a political component.

With some, especially public sector megaprojects, the link to power and politics is often very visible. Ministers want to be able to stand up and say, 'it's going to cost this much and it's going to be ready by this point'. Yet at the time of the announcement, these two things have rarely been properly worked out. A similar dynamic often plays out in the corporate sector, albeit on a less public stage.

This means that PMO leads need to be realistic in how they frame things and explicit about the uncertainty and complexity. Learning to talk about these things can be very challenging, especially for those who have grown up in a project world that has valued certainty and avoided talking about power and politics at all costs.

In a VUCA world there's no future in pretending that power and politics don't exist. In practical terms this translates into challenges around reporting and speaking truth to power – and it often overlaps with assurance.

Reporting and speaking truth to power

The PMO lead must be willing and able to speak truth to power, and the organisation must be set up to hear it. The key questions to consider are:

- What is the purpose of the reporting? Are we reporting the right things – the things that enable good decisions to be made at the right time, or are we reporting things to demonstrate compliance with things we feel 'we ought to report on'? There's a balance between paying attention to, but not being preoccupied by, the audit end of assurance with all its box ticking. Get it wrong and you can end up saying, 'we've got a report so it must be OK'.
- How do you articulate messages to land well with the different internal and external audiences? For example, when your Finance Director wants a report with detailed numbers, which the Strategy Director sees as 'four pages of complete tosh to wade through before getting to anything meaningful'.

A lot of it comes down to creating an environment where you can be truthful – even when conveying difficult messages. This means being two or three steps ahead of everyone else, and able to judge how to frame things to get the outcome you need. Say you've got a budget overrun: if you frame it well, you will get the help you need. If you get it wrong, you will set off a panic and see a raft of unintended consequences.

Creating the right environment also came up in my conversation with change management expert, Melanie Franklin, author of *Agile Change Management*.

A change manager's perspective

Melanie framed her answers to my question about the key struggles faced by change managers carefully: "Thirty years ago, if I did a change, it was like taking out a black box; some things were upstream and some downstream, but generally it was contained within a department or function. Now if I try to change one thing we're often on enterprise-wide systems; masses of people are using the same data.

"As soon as I make a change, it ripples upstream and downstream and affects stakeholders everywhere. It's hard to find all the stakeholders, let alone satisfy them. And I'm not the only one in the pond making ripples. We can be knocked sideways by the build-up of a tsunami that comes from other people changing different things around us. Their ripples just keep hitting.

"Trying to navigate through these interdependencies, and the endless stops and starts, is intellectually stretching. It's like designing a ladder for shifting sands and trying to make sure the rungs are not too far apart because people will fall through the gaps.

"The moving interdependencies make it incredibly difficult. Suddenly it's, 'we can't do this, because that one isn't finished, and we can't do that because something else isn't finished, and over there they are waiting on me'."

In this environment she identified three challenges:

- Providing reassurance
- Creating the journey planner
- Resilience and self-confidence

According to Melanie, one of these challenges stands head-and-shoulders above the others: the ability to reassure people that the change you are talking about is doable.

Providing reassurance

She explains that providing reassurance hinges on how you conduct yourself. "You have to radiate, 'I've got this; I'm going to break this down into simple steps. We're going to be able to shoehorn this change in as well. I've got a path through this, I promise.'

"It must be believable, otherwise they'll disengage. They'll say 'yes', but they won't really dig in.

"And we're operating in a minefield. Each time things change through external factors, or people stumble, your credibility takes a knock, and people lose confidence.

"When you lose credibility, everything else crumbles."

Melanie goes on to describe two other challenges that support credibility: the ability to create a journey planner and self-confidence.

Creating the journey planner

"The journey planner is like the ladder I spoke about. You use it to navigate through the interdependencies.

"The journey planner enables you to work at the macro and the micro level. At the macro level, creating it enables you to understand the ecosystem. This means going out and looking for interdependencies. Be prepared to discover that the change you are talking about is exponentially bigger than you originally thought.

"At the micro level, you need to know when to dig into the detail and how to break it down into baby steps. Each baby step will bring a sense of reward and positivity. That reward and positivity will provide the fuel and motivation to enable people to take the next step.

"Of course, it's emergent – you can't get it 100 per cent right at the outset. You must be resilient and able to forgive yourself. Holding on to the self-confidence that you are working in the right direction is another huge challenge."

Resilience and self-confidence

She continues: "Traditionally, we didn't teach project managers about resilience and self-confidence.

"For me, this means teaching emotional intelligence and developing their self-awareness and self-management. There isn't a magic bullet. They need to be able to accept that they are doing their best, and that like all humans, they will have moments of genius and moments of failure.

"They need to be flexible and resilient. When you are resilient you know that you can take whatever life throws at you. You can be open to new ideas, new experiences, new ways of doing things.

"Too often on projects, and this goes for people at all levels, from the most junior staff to board members, I see rigidity rather than flexibility. This makes sense because people are hanging on by their fingernails. And when you're stressed or scared you will defend the status quo to the end. I'm not judging them or blaming them – it's a reflection of the stress in the environment."

Takeaways

We've examined the challenges of project and programme delivery in a VUCA environment with experts from six different perspectives, and we've seen plenty of overlap in their replies.

As Gordon MacKay succinctly explained, the context in which we work has changed, and it has changed our understanding of what good project management looks like.

We might know that command and control is an out-dated approach, but we are still grappling with its legacy. It's woven into the systems, the structures and the conversations we have, and the ones we don't feel able to have, day in and day out.

It shows up when we talk about risk, and resistance to change. It shows up in governance, reporting and speaking truth to power. And it shows up in how we conduct ourselves; how we regulate ourselves emotionally; and how we inspire confidence in others over extended periods and the most trying of conditions.

Given this, it's easy to be dispirited. But I'm not!

As we change gear and move into Part 2, you'll see that understanding how the human brain works and why people behave as they do offers useful insights for dealing with every one of the 14 challenges mentioned.

References

1 Infrastructure and Projects Authority (2021), *Project Delivery Functional Standard* p47, available at: https://www.gov.uk/government/publications/ project-delivery-functional-standard (accessed: 18 October 2021)

Part 2. You, your projects and your brain

Paul Brown, co-author of *The Fear-free Organisation*, one of the first books to bring an understanding of how the human brain works to the world of organisations and change, once told me, "To understand this arena, picture a Christmas tree. There's the tree and there are the baubles. You can spend a lot of time distracted by the baubles, when it's the tree that matters."

My aim is to introduce you to the tree. However, with thousands of people researching this area every day, I have to include two health warnings. Knowledge about how the brain works is expanding all the time, and sometimes people disagree. Second, it's not possible to do justice to the complexity of the brain in a short book. What I'm presenting here is necessarily highly simplified.

This means that at times I refer to models grounded in a classical view of the brain, even though modern neuroscientists agree that the brain is a high complexity system. Lisa Feldman Barrett explains why it's important to make this distinction.

"Complexity is the metric to describe any structure that efficiently creates and transmits information. A system with high complexity can create many new patterns by combining bits and pieces of the old patterns ... The human brain is a high complexity system because, within one physical structure, it can reconfigure its billions of neurons to construct a huge repertoire of experiences, perceptions and behaviours ... This contrasts with the classical view of the brain where the different parts each accomplish a single function by themselves."[1]

3

Why people behave as they do

To make sense of 'why people behave as they do', we need a high-level understanding of how the human brain works.

As I walk you through this chapter, I am going to introduce some ideas which I suspect will be familiar and others which will be less so.

We're all familiar with the notion of the fight-and-flight response. We know that if we're under extreme pressure or exposed to threat, our fight-and-flight response will kick in. If a car comes swerving towards us down the road, we know we go into autopilot – we do what's needed to avoid the threat and to survive.

Our brain's primary concern is to ensure our survival, through a structure which can be traced back to our hunter-gatherer ancestors.

Many people are surprised to learn that the human brain does not distinguish between physical and psychological survival. It uses the same wiring to deal with physical and social threats.

Before exploring how the brain does this, I want to introduce a few ideas that may be unfamiliar.

- We're used to thinking of the brain as being confined to our heads. Well, I've news for you: it is, and it isn't.
- The brain links through the nervous system to the tips of our fingers and our toes, taking in all our organs in between.
- This brain-body combo operates a single integrated system.
- The health of this system depends on how well we manage our 'body budget'.

We'll return to these ideas later, but for now let's focus on the brain in your head.

The brain in your head

I find it helpful to visualise the brain in our head as having three key parts[2] that are intimately connected. Each has a distinct function, as shown in Figure 1.

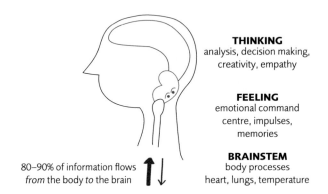

THINKING
analysis, decision making,
creativity, empathy

FEELING
emotional command
centre, impulses,
memories

BRAINSTEM
body processes
heart, lungs, temperature

80–90% of information flows
from the body *to* the brain

Figure 1 The three-part brain
Source: Visible Dynamics

- The **Brainstem** ensures body processes, such as breathing and heart function, are maintained.
- The **Feeling brain** acts as our emotional command centre. It's where aspects of memory reside, and impulsive actions begin.
- The **Thinking brain** is where higher functions originate – such as analysis, creativity, logical decision making and empathy.

I've drawn Figure 1 with a pair of eyes at the junction of the Feeling brain and Brainstem. This is to show how the brain is constantly taking in information to identify things, people and situations to avoid and conversely, those it is safe to approach.

Figure 1 also shows where the information comes from. One source is *from* your body. Read that again, because it's important and it flies in the face of what many of us believe.

Many of us believe that information flows from the brain to the body. Well, it does. But we must also take the vagus nerve into account. Amanda Blake explains, "The vagus nerve innervates the heart, gut and lungs directly. Bypassing the spinal cord, it snakes straight up the middle of the body. Between 80 and 90 per cent of the fibres in the vagus nerve send signals *to* the brain rather than receive information *from* it. Thinking of the brain as the top- down command centre is about as out-dated as thinking the world is flat."[3]

The other key source of information is your five senses (what you see, hear, taste, touch and smell). Interestingly, while you and I know when we are taking in information through our five senses, the information flow from our body to our brain is typically outside of conscious awareness.

Neuroception and emotions

This process, of the brain and nervous system working together on autopilot and outside of conscious awareness to continually assess threat levels and make judgements about what is safe and what is not, has a name – neuroception.

Stephen Porges, who coined the term, observes that we are not usually aware of the actual cues that trigger neuroception. However, we tend to be aware of the physiological shifts that result.[4] We can all recall moments when a gut-feeling, or an intuition, has told us that the context is dangerous. I'm guessing you can also recall the warm feelings and sensations that go with 'just knowing' you are safe.

We give our changing physical sensations names. They are our emotions. These sensations and the meaning we attribute to them, our emotions, drive us to act in the moment.

The avoidance response

When we're facing a real or imagined threat or danger, neuroception triggers a physical response to enable us to take avoidance action. This typically happens below our level of awareness. However, the more we learn to pay attention to our physical sensations, the easier it is to bring them into awareness and identify the associated emotions.

For example, when I feel my upper chest getting tighter and my jaw clenching, I know I'm angry. When I'm frozen to the spot, with a fluttering in my gut, I know I'm afraid. You might experience anger or fear slightly differently.

When flooded with uncomfortable sensations we have an automatic desire to discharge them. In this sense, our emotions move us to action.

Avoidance emotions, such as anger, fear, shame, disgust and sadness, lead to avoidance behaviours. When feeling threatened, we might become defensive, go on the attack, or withdraw from the situation completely.

As our survival response kicks into action, energy is diverted away from our Thinking brain. Our field of vision narrows, we become distracted, and we are less able to think clearly. Without realising it, we become preoccupied with survival.

Crucially, the brain's definition of a threat is very individual and is determined by prior experience. Working at speed, the brain doesn't stop to test whether a threat is real.

This explains why an introvert may feel put on the spot and exposed when asked for an immediate response in a review meeting, while an extrovert enjoys the opportunity to voice their views. It explains why you might become defensive on seeing a client flinch momentarily as you present performance figures, yet the same flinch has no impact on a colleague attending the same meeting.

The approach response

Not all situations provoke avoidance behaviours. Whenwe assess the situation as familiar and safe, the opposite happens. We experience physical sensations associated with pleasure and our reflex is to approach. We give these sensations names too: trust, love, excitement and joy. Emotions we tend to associate with the relationship between a mother/father and baby, rather than adults in the corporate world.

When the sensations associated with approach emotions are coursing through the body, we are highly motivated and at ease; our Thinking brain can operate at its best. We are creative, collaborative and able to learn together.

Dr Dan Siegel's terminology is helpful to contrast these two states.[5] When responding to threats, we 'flip our lid', the Thinking brain is taken 'offline' and productivity drops. When the sense of threat recedes and the flow of energy to our Thinking brain is restored, the Thinking brain comes back 'online', as shown in Figure 2.

I said earlier that the brain uses the same wiring to deal with physical and social threats. In the 21st century workplace we recognise and legislate for physical threats – just think of health and safety, for example. Yet the notion of social threat is new to most of us – despite its impact on behaviour and productivity.

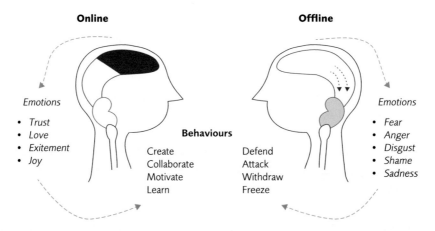

Figure 2 Emotions and behaviours change when the Thinking brain goes offline
Source: Visible Dynamics

What constitutes Social Threat?

David Rock casts light on the sources of social threat. He highlights five factors that the brain is always monitoring[6] that have a huge impact on how we behave. He summarises them with the mnemonic SCARF.

We are acutely sensitised to

Status	▪	*the perception of being considered better or worse than others*
Certainty	▪	*the predictability of future events*
Autonomy	▪	*the level of control we feel able to exert over our lives*
Relatedness	▪	*the sense of being connected to others and part of the In-group*
Fairness	▪	*the sense that we are being respected and treated fairly in comparison to others*

When people sense a change in any one of the SCARF factors, it can activate an avoidance response. The bigger the change, the stronger the response!

Picture Stefan, who has arrived on time for a performance review meeting. His new manager has been in post six weeks, yet they've spent hardly any time together. Looking through the door, Stefan sees someone else is in the room and is in the middle of a very animated conversation. The longer Stefan waits, the more unsettled he becomes.

His manager's unthinking actions have challenged his sense of status (S). As time goes on, Stefan becomes less certain (C) about what to expect and how the meeting is likely to pan out. He feels less in control of his destiny (A).

When the meeting eventually starts, Stefan's Thinking brain is not fully online. He finds it harder to gather his thoughts, hear positive feedback or think collaboratively. His manager finds him defensive.

We see and respond to social threat in the most mundane situations. These threats do not have to be explicit, intentional or real. We only have to *perceive* that our status has been reduced or that we are being treated unfairly and we will respond with avoidance behaviours.

The converse is also true. When we believe we are being treated fairly and that we have a degree of control over the future, it's easier to keep our Thinking brains online. We want the feelings of excitement and trust that come with engagement.

Understanding how the brain works adds new perspectives to many good leadership practices. Take the adage, 'When dealing with change, communicate, communicate, communicate!'

SCARF guides us to five areas that need to inform all our actions in organisational and project settings.

For example, by highlighting our desire for certainty, SCARF tells us that the prospect of change – whether a tweak to the IT system or a wholesale digital transformation – is likely to activate a threat response. We need to include this knowledge in our project planning, and make sure that we prioritise activities to reduce the degree of uncertainty and counter the threat response.

This means speaking to people about the vision for the future, and sharing plans for achieving objectives; it means explicitly discussing what you do know about the future and being willing to admit what you have yet to work out; and it means offering timescales or admitting 'we can't tell you now but we will tell you by ...'.

Figure 3 gives further examples for using SCARF in organisational and project settings.

	Activates Threat	Activates Reward
Status Importance relative to others	Asking 'Do you need advice?' Annual Performance Review Sense of being 'left out'	Noticing work done and improvements Public acknowledgement Allowing people to provide feedback on their own work
Certainty Ability to predict the future	Prospect of change Not knowing people's expectation	Vision, maps, plans and strategy Making the implicit explicit 'Can't tell you now but will tell you by...'
Autonomy Exerting control over events	Sense that stress is inescapable Pressure to conform to team norms	Having choice 'which do you prefer?' Individual 'point of need' decision-making
Relatedness Sense of safety with others	Meeting someone unkown Feeling let down or excluded	Shaking hands, swapping names, discussing something in common Showing genuine interest (listening mentoring, coaching)
Fairness Fair exchanges between people	Sense of discrimination	Increase transparency in communication Enable groups to create their own rules Help people see situation from other perspectives

Figure 3 SCARF in action
Source: Adapted from Cecil[7]

All five SCARF domains are really important. However, I believe that when it comes to projects, two of them, Certainty (and its opposite, Uncertainty) and Relatedeness (or Connection) are particularly important. We'll be taking a deeper dive into both of them later.

We've seen from this introduction to neuroscience that every interaction with another person triggers a change in the intensity and quality of our physical sensations and emotions. Most of us are unaware of these ebbs and flows. Yet, driven by our innate need to survive, they determine how we behave.

Let me say that again, as it's so important: *our physical sensations and the names we give them, our emotions, drive our behaviour*.

Now consider this. We routinely use the acronym VUCA (volatile, uncertain, complex and ambiguous), to describe the environment in which we're operating. However, I'm sure that you, like me, can think of many relationships that are VUCA too.

If you think dealing with a VUCA relationship is challenging, I widen the frame in the next chapter and add two factors that we encounter every day:

- we rarely work in isolation and
- projects are inherently stressful.

Both factors make VUCA relationships and environments more VUCA. They amplify complexity and they make project delivery even more demanding.

Takeaways

- The brain is a complex system; we cannot map specific functions onto specific parts of the brain.
- While it's useful to think of the brain having three parts: the Brainstem, the Feeling brain and the Thinking brain, it's important to think in terms of the brain-body combo.
- The brain-body combo operates a single integrated system.
- Information flows from the body to the brain, as well as from the brain to the body.
- Our physical sensations and the meaning we attribute to them, our emotions, drive us to act in the moment.
- The brain's primary concern is to ensure our survival.

- The brain does not distinguish between physical and social threat.
- Perceived threats evoke an avoidance response and take the Thinking brain offline. Feeling safe evokes an approach response and our Thinking brain stays online.
- Our emotions and behaviours change with avoidance and approach responses.
- SCARF reminds us of the five domains of social threat: Status, Certainty, Autonomy, Relatedness and Fairness.

References

1 Feldman Barrett, L. (2018), How *Emotions are Made: The Secret Life of the Brain*, London, Pan Books, p284
2 Brown, P, Kingsley, J, & Paterson, S. (2015), *The Fear-free Organisation: Vital Insights from Neuroscience to Transform Your Business Culture*, London: Kogan Page p39
3 Blake, A. (2018), *Your Body is Your Brain*, USA, Trokay Press, p50
4 Porges, S. (2017), *The Pocket Guide to the Polyvagal Theory: The Transformative Power of Feeling Safe*. New York and London, WW Norton. p19
5 Siegel, D. *(2015)*, *Dan Siegel Hand Model* available at: https://www.youtube.com/watch?v=qFTljLo1bK8 (accessed: 7 March 2018)
6 Rock, D (2009), *Managing with the Brain in Mind*, Strategy + Business, autumn 2009, Issue 56, available at: https://www.strategy-business.com/article/09306?gko=5df7f (accessed 10 March 2018)
7 Cecil in Brown, P, Kingsley, J, & Paterson, S. (2015), *The Fear-free Organisation: Vital Insights from Neuroscience to Transform Your Business Culture*, London: Kogan Page p97–98

4

Groups and stress make VUCA more VUCA

So far, we've mainly looked at interactions between two people. However, on projects things are rarely this simple. There are as many sources of social interaction and emotional triggers as people in the proverbial room (which in the modern workplace includes those we connect with digitally via email, video and social media). Emotions and behaviours are unconsciously mirrored and acted upon by others. *Group and team environments amplify emotions*. As a result, one or two anxious or frustrated individuals can have a disproportionate impact on outcomes.

The Project Stress Cycle (illustrated in Figure 4) shows how this can happen through the story of Fred. As you read it, bear in mind that stress is not a bad thing per se. But before we get to that, let's spend a few moments understanding stress and arousal.

Stress and arousal: finding the balance for optimal performance

We've known since the early 1900s that there is a relationship between the brain's level of arousal and our ability to perform a task. The Yerkes-Dodson law of performance shows an inverted U curve. When we have lots of time and little to do, we can find it hard to focus and performance suffers. The brain needs a degree of stimulation to operate at its best.

Too much arousal makes us stressed, anxious and even overwhelmed. It takes our Thinking brain offline. We lose the ability to focus, we have less emotional control and we are easily triggered into avoidance behaviours. However, there is a middle ground towards the top of the inverted U where, with 'just the right amount of arousal', our Thinking Brain stays online. We are focused, creative and motivated by a cascade of reward emotions.

The vicious circle of excess stress and declining performance

The Project Stress Cycle

Picture Fred, a senior member of the project team. Things are not going his way. He's getting increasingly frazzled. He is holding it together but doesn't realise how stressed he is. He is snapping at everyone and he's finding it harder to act in a rational manner.

The impact on those around him is palpable. No one wants to provoke an outburst, so they give him a wide berth. And of course, after a bruising meeting

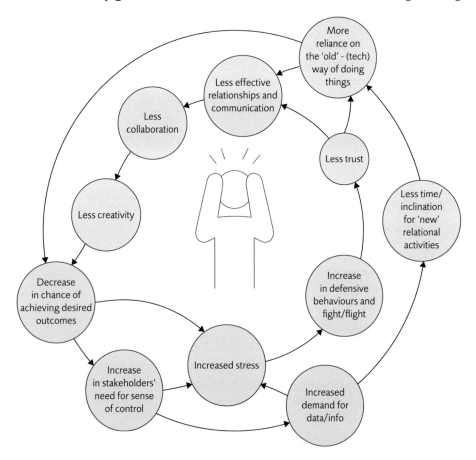

Figure 4 The Project Stress Cycle[1]
Source: Visible Dynamics

it's hard to keep your own Thinking brain online. Trust is falling across the piece and relationships and communication are suffering.

When the project started, Fred and his colleagues went out of their way to highlight the need to invest time in building relationships and ensuring people worked well together. They repeatedly reminded the team that 'successful delivery relies on collaboration and creativity'.

But now the pressure is on and metrics are the primary focus. As relationships get strained, collaboration is more difficult. Rather than waste time struggling to work together, people are falling back into old habits and old silos. They are relying on approaches that worked in the past. But without quality collaboration, it's hard to be truly creative.

And the word on the street? The project is unlikely to achieve the desired outcomes – which does nothing for stress levels.

Powerful stakeholders are getting nervous. They are demanding more and more information in slightly different formats to reassure themselves that things are under control. These demands distract the team from the work they should be doing and add to the stress.

They have less time and less inclination to work collaboratively, and the preoccupation with spreadsheets and metrics is forcing them to adopt behaviours that reduce the chance of success and multiply stress – right across the system.

The key message is that we need to be alert to *excess stress* because it can trigger a cycle that plays out across the wider project system and impacts delivery.

Some projects slide into stress cycles at crunch points (gateway reviews, for example). Others can be in a chronic state of stress for years – chewing up and spitting out those charged with delivery.

None of this is surprising when seen through the lens of neuroscience. Especially when we consider the powerful stakeholders involved, the scale of investment, and the private and organisational reputations at stake.

Our innate need to belong increases complexity

In telling the story of Fred, I have illustrated how the behaviour of one person can increase the complexity of delivery. Yet even this is a simplification of what happens in real life. In real life, as soon as we get into team and group environments, another source of complexity comes to the fore – our innate need to belong.

When we are in team and group environments we become sensitive to any indication, real or imagined, that we will be ostracised or ejected. (Remember the S for status and R for relatedness in SCARF).

This fear, albeit unconscious, has an impact on the dynamics. We'll see when we discuss psychological safety that it can create a climate where people are afraid to speak up.

It also makes us more inclined to go along with irrational decisions and dysfunctional behaviour, and it explains why groupthink can be so powerful; groupthink preserves that crucial sense of belonging – even if doing so works against the best interests of project delivery.

If this isn't enough to make you take neuroscience seriously, look at the impact of the stress cycle on culture and mental health when the quest for high performance is taken to extremes.

High performance can turn toxic

"We asked about building high performance project teams and found a recurring theme of brutal cultures and mental health issues. Teams in bigger and more complex projects often have a battle rhythm characterised by cognitive overload, decision fatigue, day-in-day-out conflict and excessive stress. This results in poor mental health or even PTSD-like symptoms."[2]

Collin Smith was summarising the findings of the ICCPM's 2018 Roundtable research into leadership and complex projects.[3] He went on: "Unfortunately, there's a trend: leaders in these projects keep pushing and pushing – to the detriment of their own mental health and that of their teams. And productivity suffers.

"Although these project leaders are responsible for monitoring staff wellbeing, at times they seem to exhibit a pride in the scar tissue they've acquired over decades. They tend to batten down the hatches, crack the whip and crank up the stress to get things done.

"Yet our research tells us, when complex projects really get tough, the opposite is needed. We need leaders at their very best in terms of critical thinking, creativity, collaboration and adaptability.

"We need leaders who, despite the overload and stress, can slow down rather than becoming more transactional and process-driven."

What do we conclude? Project organisations recognise stress and know it needs managing. However, the ICCPM's research showed that the approach taken by many organisations to do this (giving project leaders responsibility for managing wellbeing) often doesn't work.

In my view, the reason for this is clear. This approach doesn't work because it is too simplistic. It doesn't take into account how the human brain works, or systemic dynamics like the Project Stress Cycle.

The dynamics of brutal cultures

The human fight/flight response evolved to help our ancestors cope with intermittent periods of high stress – not the unrelenting pressures of organisational life. Add to this the high stakes and high risks associated with major projects and we can see why problems arise.

Lacking the opportunity to de-stress, many of the project leaders Collin was referring to will be in a wired state of hypervigilance. Like a bird in the garden that suspects a cat is on the prowl, they will be in overdrive looking out for things they need to avoid. Anything is better than getting caught out.

In other words, their Thinking brains are offline. And when Thinking brains are offline, we see things less clearly. If we can't really see what's going on, we start making assumptions about what is actually happening.

The fight/flight reflex says it all. If we're not going to run away, we may well start fighting. And of course, that increases stress levels across the team – it makes a brutal culture far more brutal.

If you want to create a culture of high performance, you have to take the human fight/flight response into account and actively nurture a group phenomenon known as psychological safety.

Psychological safety, the antidote to a toxic culture, boosts all aspects of performance

Psychological safety is: "The belief that the work environment is safe for interpersonal risk taking ... feeling able to speak up with relevant ideas, questions or concerns. It is present when colleagues trust and respect each other and feel able – even obligated – to be candid."[4]

This definition, from Amy Edmondson, is deceptively simple, and its ramifications profound.

Think of the organisations, project teams and leaders you know. How many demonstrate a disconnect between aspiration and reality? They want to be known for delivering great results and finding creative solutions. Yet many just get stuck because of invisible dynamics that play out on a daily basis.

You see it when a team member keeps quiet even though they can see something is clearly going wrong. You see it when a contractor doesn't mention a different way of working in case they get laughed at. And you see it in ritualised board meetings and team meetings where groupthink prevails or the risk of being cast as the dissenting voice is just too high.

When psychological safety is low, we secretly fear being punished, humiliated or ostracised for speaking the truth as we see it. Low psychological safety gets in the way of team performance and project delivery. And, when you can't deliver the outcomes you've promised, it gets in the way of personal success.

If you are wondering about the evidence, take a look at Edmondson's book *The Fearless Organization*. It includes numerous case studies, including Google's Project Aristotle.

Researching team effectiveness: Project Aristotle

Project Aristotle was a multi-year research programme that set out to identify what makes Google's most effective project teams so effective. "Led by Julia Rozovsky, the researchers considered people's educational backgrounds, hobbies, friends, personality traits and more, in their analysis set of 180 teams from all over the company. They found nothing. No mix of personality types or skills or backgrounds emerged that helped explain which teams performed well and which didn't. It seemed like there was no answer to the question of why some teams thrive and others fail." Until they came across the concept of psychological safety and "'everything suddenly fell into place'. What they had discovered was that even the extremely smart, high powered employees at Google needed a psychologically safe work environment to contribute the talent they had to offer.[5]

"The researchers found that what really mattered was less about who is on the team, and more about how the team worked together. In order of importance:

Psychological safety	▪ *team members feel safe to take risks and be vulnerable in front of each other*
Dependability	▪ *team members get things done on time and meet Google's high bar for excellence*
Structure and clarity	▪ *team members have clear roles, plans, and goals*
Meaning of the work	▪ *work is personally important to team members*
Impact of work	▪ *team members think their work matters and creates change"[6]*

Notably, as Rosovsky put it, "'psychological safety was by far the most important... it was the underpinning of the other four'."

Psychological safety is the key enabler for building a high performance culture. It is not soft or about being nice. It is about creating a climate that is characterised by trust and respect, so that people feel safe to take interpersonal risks. It is the antidote to the brutality identified by Collin Smith on page 36.

Did you spot the *interpersonal* risk in the last paragraph? Risk management gets lots of attention in projects. But its main focus is on risks 'out there'. How much time do you spend talking, or even explicitly thinking, about personal risk? I'm not alluding to the risk appetite of key stakeholders (even though that is important). I'm talking about what each of us personally sees, and experiences, as risky in our dealings with others. For example, what do you do with that momentary thought, 'dare I push back?' when the finance director challenges your figures at a project board meeting? Do you stop to consider possibilities, or do you rule it out immediately?

I want to divert the discussion for a moment from psychological safety (a group phenomenon), to focus on your attitude to personal risk. Whatever your answer to the question, 'dare I push back?', I suspect you'll gain additional insight through considering your response in the context of the next section, on mindsets.

Encouraging a learning project team: the Growth Mindset

The term Growth Mindset was coined by Carol Dweck to explain why some children love learning and readily embrace new challenges while others, those with a Fixed Mindset, are wary of new challenges and actively avoid them. Her subsequent research showed that these two terms apply to people at large.

According to Dweck, at its simplest, people with a Fixed Mindset believe that human qualities such as intellectual skills are carved in stone and not open to change; you either have them or you don't. This belief brings 'an urgency to prove yourself ... it simply wouldn't do to look or feel deficient'. People with a Fixed Mindset tend to evaluate every situation with questions like, 'Will I succeed or fail? Will I be accepted or rejected?'. They are fearful of new challenges because of the inherent risk. 'If I make a mistake, I'll show my shortcomings, and that would be a bad thing'.

People with a Growth Mindset believe that 'human qualities are things to be cultivated through effort, strategies and help from others. Yes, people start in different places, but everyone can change and grow through application and experience.'[7] This brings a completely different attitude to success and failure. Success is about growing and developing. Failure is something you learn from – it's vital for future growth. New challenges are to be embraced, not avoided.

Think about yourself for a moment, at work, at home, with your family, with hobbies – where do you have a Growth Mindset, and where do you have a Fixed Mindset? What is, or was, encouraged? What impact has that had?

Now think about your projects – what's encouraged, and what are you encouraging? Can you see how that relates to psychological safety?

I said earlier that psychological safety is a group phenomenon. We need to actively cultivate it, so that everyone can keep their Thinking Brains online. Figure 5 shows psychological safety is a pre-requisite for creativity, collaboration and learning. Without it, we inadvertently trigger avoidance behaviours and add to the complexity of delivery.

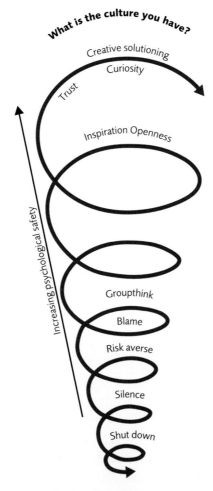

Figure 5 The spiral of psychological safety

Source: Adapted from Uenlinotes[8]

Psychological safety is dynamic and emergent – it depends very much on what's going on in the external environment, who is in the team and what is happening for them. We cannot assume that just because psychological safety was high six weeks ago, we will stay at the top of the spiral.

The NeuroLeadership Institute (NLI) puts a slightly different spin on the same terrain. They speak about the need for a Growth Mindset Culture where "most, if not all, employees hold the dual belief that improvement is both *possible* and the *purpose* of the work employees do ... They uplift one another, welcome new ideas, and strive to get better. They do not point fingers, shut people down, or assert themselves as geniuses."[9]

It doesn't matter whether we are talking about psychological safety or a Growth Mindset Culture – both need deliberate fostering. In Part 3, I discuss how, and in Part 4, look at several projects that have done so. But first, I want to summarise where we've got to, and to look at what this means in practical terms.

When we understand how the human brain works, it becomes obvious that creating and nurturing psychological safety, i.e. a fear-free environment, is key to successful project delivery – no matter what your job title.

This means:

- Learning to recognise and contain your emotions in order to keep your Thinking brain online. (Note: I'm saying contain, not ignore them! More on this in Part 3).
- With Thinking brain online, you'll be:
  □ better able to contain the emotions of those you interact with directly, and indirectly, (your customers, team, sponsors, stakeholders and suppliers);
  □ better equipped to read the situation clearly;
  □ less likely to trigger a threat response in others, and
  □ able to respond flexibly to retrieve the situation on the occasions when you do.

We saw that emotions are contagious, and the stress cycle illustrated just how quickly things can get out of hand.

Remember my observation on page 34; the story of Fred illustrates how the behaviour of one person can increase the complexity of delivery, and this is a simplification of what happens in real life where many people are involved.

Put all this together and the bottom line is clear.

If you're not *intentionally* nurturing psychological safety, the way the human brain works means that you will unwittingly be making a VUCA world more VUCA, adding to complexity and reducing the chances of successful delivery.

Whatever your role, you need the skills to counter the pull to complexity.

Takeaways

- Groups and team environments amplify emotions.
- Our innate need to belong increases complexity.
- Excess stress can trigger a cycle that plays out across the wider project system and adversely impacts delivery.
- We need leaders who, despite the overload and stress, can slow down rather than becoming more transactional and process driven. Those who don't, run the risk of creating a toxic environment where high performance is impossible to achieve.
- Individuals with a Growth Mindset believe everyone can change and grow, failure is something you learn from, and new challenges are to be embraced. The opposite is true for those with a Fixed Mindset.
- Creating a high-performance culture means actively nurturing psychological safety, to support interpersonal risk-taking/a Growth Mindset Culture.
- If you're not *intentionally* cultivating psychological safety, you will unwittingly be adding to complexity by making a VUCA world more VUCA – and reducing the chances of successful delivery.
- We all need the skills to counteract this pull to complexity.

References

1 Osterweil, C. (2019), *Project Delivery, Uncertainty and Neuroscience, a Leader's Guide to Walking in Fog*, UK, Visible Dynamics, p25
2 ICCPM and Visible Dynamics (2020), *Stress, Culture and High-Performance Project Teams*, available at: https://soundcloud.com/user-680350226/stress_culture_high_performance_project_teams (accessed 10 June 2021)
3 ICCPM International Roundtable Series (2018), *Project Leadership: the game-changer in large scale complex projects.* available at: https://iccpm.com/project-leadership/(accessed 31 July 2019)

4 Edmondson, A. (2019), *The Fearless Organization: creating psychological safety in the workplace for learning innovation and growth*, New Jersey, Wiley p8

5 Edmondson, A. (2019), *The Fearless Organization: creating psychological safety in the workplace for learning innovation and growth*, New Jersey, Wiley p41.

6 Identify dynamics of effective teams, available at https://rework.withgoogle.com/guides/understanding-team-effectiveness/steps/identify-dynamics-of-effective-teams/(accessed 22 March 2022)

7 Dweck, C, *Mindset: The New Psychology of Success*, Chap 1-3, available at: https://dci.stanford.edu/wp-content/uploads/2018/03/mindset-chap-1-3.pdf (accessed 12 September 2021)

8 Image source: Uenlinotes(2020), *Psychological Safety*, available at https://voynetch.com/4651 (accessed: 1 November 2020)

9 Neuroleadership Institute (2021), *Impact Report: Growth Mindset Supports Organisations Through Disruption*, available at: https://hub.neuroleadership.com/growth-mindset-impact-report (accessed 11 September 2021)

5

Skills that everybody needs

We closed Chapter 4 talking about having the skills to counter the pull towards complexity. In my view, success in a VUCA world hinges on you having the self-awareness to know when your Thinking brain is going offline; and the know-how, or self-management, to do something about it when it does.

I see these two skills as foundation stones. If you've come across emotional intelligence, you'll recognise them – self-awareness and self-management are the foundations of emotional intelligence, too.

Getting the most from yourself: emotional intelligence redefined

The term emotional intelligence gained traction in the 1990s with publication of Daniel Goleman's book of the same name. Since then, we've seen the development of many models of emotional intelligence, typically comprising lists of competences. Goleman offers a list of 12, split into four domains.[1]

- **Self awareness**
  - □ emotional self awareness
- **Self management**
  - □ emotional self control
  - □ adaptability
  - □ achievement orientation
  - □ positive outlook
- **Social awareness**
  - □ empathy
  - □ organisational awareness
- **Relationship management**
  - □ influence
  - □ conflict management

Neuroscience for project success

- ☐ teamwork
- ☐ coaching and mentoring
- ☐ inspirational leadership

I find these lists of competences of limited use and prefer to link the four domains to the earlier discussion of how the human brain works using the powerful questions shown in Figure 6.

We start in the top left, looking inside ourselves with the question:
- How online is my Thinking brain?

Once we've answered this, we can turn our attention to self-regulation and self-management:
- How do I get my Thinking brain online/more online?

Then we're ready to move on to others and look outside with the follow-up questions:
- How online are their Thinking brains?
- How do I get their Thinking brains online/more online?

Finally, we add two more questions about building sustainability:
- How do I keep my Thinking brain online?
- How do I keep their Thinking brains online?

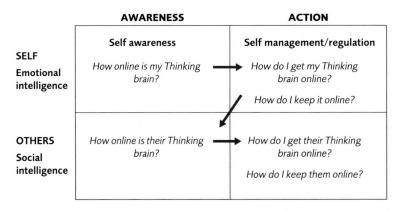

Figure 6 Emotional intelligence as questions

Source: Visible Dynamics

Our emotional and social intelligence relies on our ability to answer the central question: 'How online is my Thinking brain?', so it's vital that we all learn to recognise when our Thinking brain is going offline and develop the skill to bring it back online.

You may be surprised that the ability to do this has a name – it's 'being mindful'.

Many leaders I work with find the notion of 'being mindful' difficult to grasp, and some prefer to talk about 'being present'. Others glaze over at both terms because they sound too new-age. If this is you, the concept of 'cognitive readiness' (introduced on page 60) provides an alternative framing. Whatever your preference, let's explore what I'm talking about.

The skill of being mindful

What do we mean by being mindful?

Professor Mark Williams of Oxford University explains that, when you are mindful, you have: "a direct, intuitive knowing of what you are doing while you are doing it. You know what's going on *inside* your mind and body, and what's going on in the outside world as well.

"Most of the time our attention is not where we intend it to be. Our attention is hijacked by our thoughts and emotions, by our concerns, by our worries for the future, and our regrets and memories of the past. *Developing mindful awareness is about learning to pay attention, in the present moment, and without judgement. It's like training a muscle – training attention to be where you want it to be.* This reduces our tendency to work on autopilot, allowing us to choose how we respond and react."[2]

Read that again. How much of the time is your attention where you intend it to be? How much is spent going over things from the past? Perhaps you're allocating blame (including to yourself) or wondering how you could have done it differently. How much of the time are you here, but not as present, confident and assertive as you'd like to be? If so, perhaps there are moments when you feel a bit frozen, like a rabbit caught in the headlights. How much time is spent with your head in the future – creating numerous scenarios about what's going to happen next and how you'll respond if it does?

I'm not suggesting that you should never look back to learn lessons or that you should never look forward and plan. But I am encouraging you to consider whether there are occasions when you spend too much time and energy ruminating and turning the same thoughts over again and again.

Is it possible that sometimes you are caught up in fantasy? A fantasy that fuels your stress levels, takes your Thinking brain offline and may even keep you up at night? Is it possible that sometimes the frozen feeling is an indication that your Thinking brain is not fully online?

If you've answered yes to any of these questions, you'll be wondering if you can learn to get your Thinking brain online.

My answer is, yes you can. You do it by developing your mindful awareness muscle. Your mindful awareness muscle tells you what you *do* know about *yourself* and the *external world* (as opposed to fantasies about yourself and the external world). A strong mindful awareness muscle can give you access to data that you are not routinely aware of.

Your mindful awareness muscle

I suspect the idea of a mindful awareness muscle sounds a bit abstract. I'll explain how to find yours with the help of a Pilates class.

Locating your mindful awareness muscle: the Pilates class

A few years ago, I won a private Pilates class in an auction. Now, I don't do Pilates, but I remember the lesson very clearly.

In fact, I'm back there now – lying on the sitting room floor with the instructor towering over me. "I want you to raise your legs using your stomach muscles." I frowned. "Run that by me again."

"Raise your legs using your stomach muscles," she repeated.

I frowned again – I had no idea what she was talking about.

I tried to explain, "It's no good, you have to come down here and show me where those muscles are."

She bent down and tapped my belly. "Ah, that's where they are – the muscles that connect my stomach to my legs!"

I've used them many times since that day. I still wouldn't call myself an expert (I don't do nearly enough repetitions), but at least I know what's possible.

I find it helpful to think about my mindful awareness muscle as being just like all my other muscles. If you've studied anatomy, you may know their names. But I suspect that many of you, like me in the Pilates class, are not that sophisticated.

The Pilates teacher wanted me to use a particular group of muscles, but I couldn't. I had no idea how to locate them. The same happened with my mindful awareness muscle – 10 years ago, I didn't know I had one.

The good news is, once you've located your mindful awareness muscle, you can start to use it. And as with any muscle, the more you use it the stronger it will get.

Of course, the mindful awareness muscle doesn't exist – it's a metaphor. It's a wonderful way of considering how your thoughts, emotions and physical sensations link up. And as you learn to do this you will develop the ability to access data that previously would have been out of reach.

Let's go back to that quote from Mark Williams. The emphasis is on not letting our attention get hijacked by memories of the past, or fantasies about the future. In the next sections we'll explore memories from the past and fantasies for the future in more depth – knowing that when we master them with a strong mindful awareness muscle, we'll be able to see what is going on now with real clarity. And this will enable us to be truly present.

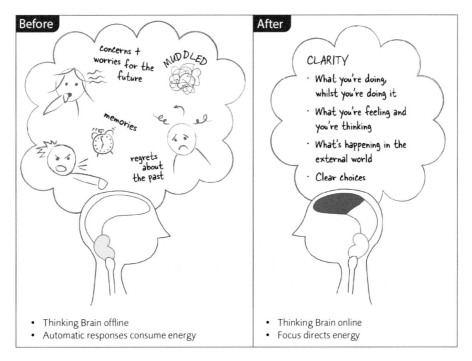

Figure 7 Why develop your mindful awareness muscle?

Source: Visible Dynamics

Echoes from the past – how memory works

To truly understand what 'not getting caught by memories from the past' means, we need to unpick the notion of memory and understand that there are two key types of memory – explicit and implicit. We don't make this distinction in everyday conversation, but it's important to know the differences.

Types of memory

Usually when we talk about memory we're referring to explicit memory. Explicit memories are 'things which come easily to mind', including people, facts, objects, places and events. When we access them we have a *sense of recalling something*. For example, if I ask you what you did on a particular date, say last Friday, or your son's birthday. You can open your mental filing cabinet and flick through the folders, until you get to the right one.

Implicit memories are different. They are the 'things we know, but we don't know we know them'; they reside in the non-conscious mind. Often automatic, they can *pop into awareness for no apparent reason*.[3] Implicit memories include images, feelings, habits and the sensory, body-based skills that support automatic, unconscious actions – just think of riding a bike or cleaning your teeth. They come with a felt-sense.

Amanda Blake describes it this way in her book, *Your Body is Your Brain*: "When accessing implicit memory *you don't feel as if you are remembering* anything at all ... it feels like you just do what comes naturally. In fact doing anything else usually provokes discomfort and a sense of 'I couldn't possibly do that'. You're on autopilot."[4]

Implicit memory is a fantastic resource. Yet the very fact it comes with autopilot can be problematic.

Consider your projects for a moment. Have you ever seen someone behaving in a way that seems disproportionate or makes little sense? Perhaps a stakeholder or team member lost their rag, or panicked over a minor detail.

Have *you* ever been that person? I know I have, on more than one occasion! And each time, I struggled to fathom out what had been going on, until one incident, a driving lesson, enabled me to pull the strands together.

The driving lesson – when autopilot goes wrong

My daughter was learning to drive and needed to practise, so I was in the passenger seat on a quiet Sunday afternoon. She was doing pretty well.

We approached the junction, she checked the mirror, slowed down and indicated to turn left. She brought the car to halt, and with no traffic ahead, nosed out onto the hill. All textbook stuff.

Then it happened, blind panic – mine not hers. My stomach was in my mouth, my heart pounding. "You've got to stop. Pull in. Pull in!" I screeched.

She did as I asked, and a few seconds later we were stationary at the side of the road, my panic subsiding. I couldn't explain what had caused it.

But I knew two things. Something had sent my Thinking brain wildly offline and there had been nothing wrong with her driving.

I spent a long time afterwards puzzling about what had happened and trying to work out what was behind that feeling of panic. Something about the sensation of my stomach rising to my mouth was familiar. But I couldn't put a finger on it.

Weeks later, I was walking the dog and thinking about nothing in particular when it fell into place. An image from 20 years earlier came to mind.

I was in the front seat of a taxi in the Himalayas. The road was narrow and the taxi driver, I remembered, had a penchant for turning off the engine and cruising in neutral. At the same time he'd turn his head to see my response, delighting in my discomfort at the steep drops and hairpin bends. I tried to keep my cool. What could I, an unaccompanied female in the middle of nowhere, do?

At one point he switched off the engine and the keys fell into the foot tray. He bent down and grappled for them by my feet.

That was it, the Aha moment! The driving lesson's sensation of rising panic was familiar because I'd experienced it before – during the taxi ride when, one hand in the foot tray, other hand on the wheel, the driver had twisted around to grin at me.

What can we learn from this story?

Did you spot that I spent a long time puzzling about what had happened, yet the Aha moment came when I was thinking about something else and walking the dog?

Aha moments

The authors of *The Fear-free Organization* explain Aha moments this way: "All seemingly spontaneous ideas or acts of creativity involve neural firing that connects current thoughts with past experience ... they depend on subtle connections between things that may, on the conscious surface, not appear to be connected at all."[5].

They go on to say that it's counterintuitive: "The harder we concentrate on coming up with inspirational ideas the more frustrated we are likely to become ... [The Aha moment] is the culmination of ideas that have been simmering on the brain's back burner, perhaps for quite a long period of time. Trying to pull them together inhibits the flow."

Often we work too hard at problem solving when what's needed is the mental space to create links.

Once I got that space, I could piece together the fragments of image, feelings and sensation, and link them to specific events. I had a clear explanation of what had happened: something about the way my daughter was driving must have evoked an echo of what it felt like in the taxi. My guess is the car was in neutral for a second or two, and that, combined with the narrow road and the hill triggered me – it took me instantaneously back to the Himalayas.

Triggers and mental filing

Think about those times when your behaviour (or someone else's) has seemed inappropriate or disproportionate. Could triggering explain it?

In this instance, I've made the connection and can see how, in the context of the taxi ride, my blind panic during the driving lesson makes perfect sense. Essentially my brain has taken the two events and the associated implicit memories, and successfully filed them away.

Now the filing has been done, I'm unlikely to be caught out in the same way. Next time I will recognise that sensation in my stomach for what it is – an echo of the past.

Dan Siegel explains that the act of mental filing utilises a part of the brain called the hippocampus. He describes the hippocampus as: "a master puzzle piece assembler, which draws together separate pieces of images and sensations of implicit memory into the assembled 'pictures' of factual and autobiographical memory."[6] He goes on to explain that this hippocampal work makes the 'search engine' of explicit memory retrieval more efficient, but it requires focused attention.

Some things, including moments of intense emotions, such as terror (my taxi ride), rage and exposure to high levels of stress over extended periods, can take our hippocampus offline. When this happens, the jigsaw pieces of implicit memory remain free-floating, 'in unassembled neural disarray'. And, as in the driving lesson, they have the ability to come from nowhere and trigger behaviours that make no sense to an external observer.

Imperfect mental filing and the associated free-floating, implicit memory fragments also explain the flashbacks and PTSD-like issues identified in the ICCPM research on page 36.

I've told this story to give you an understanding of how memory works and how it can trigger unexpected behaviours. I am also hoping it will encourage you to reflect on your own experiences and behaviour. As you do so, it's important to remember *we always behave the way we do for very good reason* – even if, on occasion the reasons are so hard to fathom that we need external help to piece the jigsaw together.

You may have noticed that we're beginning to touch on mental health, a subject that I know can be challenging. I'm conscious that you may be tempted to dismiss it as irrelevant or too difficult. Before you do, can I encourage you to stop for a moment?

Research means that our understanding of how the human mind works is moving at great speed. There is now plenty of scientific evidence to suggest that it no longer makes sense to treat mental and physical health as two completely separate entities; we need to pay more attention to the brain-body combo.[7]

Promoting mental health

In *A Question of Leadership*, Keith Leslie, chair of the Samaritans, challenges us to consider that *promoting mental health is a leadership opportunity*.[8] He observes: "In recent years we've come to understand that:

- We are all on a continuum of mental health, just as we are with physical health – more or less mentally fit and healthy from time to time.
- Our experiences and our environment are primary factors in our mental health every day, far outweighing the impact of heredity or biochemistry."

That second statement, highlighting the impact of our daily experiences and environment, signposts the link to project culture.

He goes on to scotch a few myths and clarify how we can promote mental health at work. I've summarised his key points in Figure 8. I believe his observation, 'It's not about becoming a therapist', speaks to the fears of many.

It's not about	■ Reducing the challenge of work – good challenge at work improves mental health
	■ Becoming a therapist to your people – this requires specialist skills – but there is still plenty we can do
	■ Avoiding the subject of promoting mental health at work – doing so works against creating a healthy workplace
It's about	■ Becoming more productive and more flexible
	■ Improving motivation and performance
	■ Investing in resilience, support and equipping line managers
	■ Grasping the nettle of unacceptable behaviour

Figure 8 Scotching myths about mental health at work

We'll see in Part 4 how promoting mental health and wellbeing was central to work on one project, The Belfast Transport Hub. We'll also see how this stood them in good stead as they contended with the pandemic.

You may have noticed that during the pandemic mental health rocketed up the agenda. The mass move to working from home (WfH) contributed to this. It also shone a spotlight onto the challenges of remote working, highlighted a chasm between good and poor practice, and introduced a raft of new issues for organisations and leaders to deal with.

Anne Archer, mental health advocate, explains why so many of us found WfH so difficult: "Humans have a fundamental, biological need for connection that's human to human, face to face and in the same room. We can't get away from the fact that many people really struggle without it. We underestimate the difference it makes to mental health, wellbeing and productivity. When there isn't an opportunity to be physically together in the same room, we must seriously consider what we can do to give people the best feeling of connection, so no one feels invisible."[9]

Remember the discussions earlier about psychological safety, our innate need to belong and the 'R', relatedness, in the SCARF framework? Here they are again, this time in the context of mental health. In Part 3 many of the tools I introduce help promote that vital sense of connection.

If you need further evidence of the business case for using them, a report by Deloitte, published in January 2020, included two statistics that may surprise. In the UK the estimated annual costs to employers of poor mental health is £45bn, and employers obtain an average return of £5 for every £1 invested in initiatives to improve mental health[10] – and that was *before* the pandemic.

Fantasies of the future: fears that undermine performance

Let's return to the quote from Mark Williams on page 47 and consider the moments when "our attention is hijacked by our concerns, our worries for the future".

I challenged you earlier to consider how much of your time and energy goes into creating endless scenarios about what might happen and how to deal with them. I used to do exactly the same, until someone named the pattern. I was trying to be a mind reader! That brought me up short.

The brain is an anticipatory machine, constantly scanning and trying to predict what will come next. These predictions are formulated below our level of awareness and they change from moment to moment.

You may remember an advert that came out years ago. It starts with a skinhead running towards the camera. Every time I saw it, it would trigger a deep sense of apprehension and disquiet in me.

The camera angle changes, an elderly man shuffles into view and my suspense increased. We glimpse a corrugated roof – sliding. The skinhead dives forwards. My heart was in my mouth.

The camera angle changes again. The skinhead intercepts the roof to protect the old man. Phew! (I get the same adrenaline rush writing about it today, as I did when the advert first came out).

I'm telling you this to illustrate how our feelings and predictions change in real time as we pick up new information and evaluate it through the process of neuroception. Dan Siegel puts it this way: "Our readiness for response is enhanced by anticipating the next moment in time – what the world may offer next and what behaviour to initiate in response."[11]

When you get caught up in fantasising about what might happen, are you endeavouring to be a mind reader and attempting to second guess every eventuality?

If so, you will find it helpful to remember two points about emotions:

- Emotions and the associated physical sensations rise and fall, like the waves on the sea. If you wait long enough, and don't engage with them, difficult emotions will subside.
- The difficult emotions associated with anticipating an event are typically far more intense than the emotions we experience during the event itself. This

happens because we can wind ourselves up just thinking about what's to come. Then we project what we *imagine* we will feel onto the event, and this makes it seem even worse.

Knowing this helps me keep perspective. I've come to realise that frenetic mindreading and generating multiple scenarios are indications that my Thinking brain is offline.

The trick is to recognise this for what it is (an avoidance response in overdrive), and then to do something to bring your Thinking brain back online. This is where learning to be more mindful comes in.

Learning to be more mindful

I said earlier that many in the project world find the notion of mindfulness difficult to grasp. In recent months when running online workshops and webinars I've polled several hundred project leaders to find out what they know about the subject. I've asked the same question: "When it comes to mindfulness, which of these responses applies to you?"

1. I've embraced it wholeheartedly
2. I've dabbled a bit
3. I'm not sure it works for me
4. It's passed me by

I've had consistent results. Around four per cent say that mindfulness has passed them by; 60 per cent report that they have dabbled a bit; seven per cent are not sure it works for them, while the remaining 25 per cent say they have embraced it wholeheartedly.

When I explore what's behind these answers, I often discover that people confuse being more mindful with meditation. They are not the same thing.

Don't confuse being mindful with meditation

Mindfulness is a *quality*; meditation is a *practice*.

"Mindfulness is the basic human ability to be fully present, aware of where we are and what we're doing, and not overly reactive or overwhelmed by what's going on around us."[12]

In contrast, "Meditation is the act of giving your attention to only one thing, either as a religious activity or as a way of becoming calm and relaxed."[13]

If you are like me, you will have grown up associating meditation with religious and spiritual traditions. I assumed meditating meant sitting quietly for long periods of time and I believed it had no relevance in my world. In recent years I've discovered my assumptions were inaccurate and my understanding of, and interest in, meditation has grown – especially as the scientific research into the benefits of meditating has increased.

Research shows that when we train the brain to be mindful, we are also changing its physical structure. For example, after an eight-week course of mindful meditation practice, MRI scans show that the parts of the brain associated with fear, emotion and the body's response to stress, appear to shrink, as if it becomes less activated. At the same time the prefrontal cortex [associated with awareness, attention and decision making] – i.e. the Thinking brain – becomes thicker. What's more, the connections between the parts of the brain associated with stress and the rest of the brain get weaker, while the connections between the areas associated with attention get stronger.[14]

While mindful meditation is a highly effective route to developing your mindful awareness muscle, it is not the only one. In Part 3 I offer some exercises to help you create 'mindful moments' which bring you into the present. When you know how, there arc plenty of activities like yoga, playing a musical instrument, walking in nature, stroking a pet or painting a picture that are helpful.

In fact, you are being mindful and developing your mindful awareness muscle "whenever you bring awareness to what you're directly experiencing via your senses, or to your state of mind via your thoughts and emotions".[15]

What matters is learning to get out of your head!

If this all sounds far removed from the day-to-day reality of projects, I want to bring you back to something you have to do, whatever your role: weigh up risks and make decisions when you are uncertain about the best way forward.

Risk assessment and decision making

It doesn't matter if we are talking about the Risks (with a capital 'R') dissected in business case reviews and governance meetings, or risks of the 'dare I say what I really think?' variety, the principles are the same.

We like to think our decisions are completely rational and informed by conscious situational assessments such as: 'Have I seen this before? What do I know about it? What data do I need to make a judgement call?'

However, if there's an element of uncertainty, conscious situational assessments are only part of the story when it comes to weighing up risks and decision making. Ruth Murray-Webster and Eleanor Winton explain that there are two other inputs, both subconscious, that have a big impact. Both are driven by our innate, human drive to survive:[16]

- automatic reactions, driven by subconscious mental shortcuts (heuristics) and cognitive biases and
- raw, visceral emotions.

You may have come across research into heuristics and cognitive biases and the lists of the types of mental shortcut we make. For example:

- the availability heuristic: the most recent memories of events are the most memorable and we are biased to believe they will happen again;
- the representative heuristic: we make snap judgements because people and situations seem familiar and we assume that in certain situations they are likely to behave in a certain way;
- optimism bias: our tendency to overestimate the likelihood of experiencing positive events and underestimate the likelihood of experiencing negative events in the future;
- confirmation bias: our tendency to process and analyse information in such a way that it supports our pre-existing ideas and convictions.

I'll leave you to look up other heuristics and cognitive biases because it's the third category, raw, visceral emotion, that interests me.

Why? Because raw, visceral emotions, discussed in a matter-of-fact way, do not get much airtime in routine project and organisational conversations. Yet they have been shown to have some of the biggest impacts on our decision making.

If you are interested in decision making, it's important to realise that these three sets of influences are interwoven into a triple strand, see Figure 9. At the point of making a decision, a person or decision-making group doesn't know for certain what's driving their behaviour.[17]

Ruth and Eleanor emphasise: "Most of the time in daily life this doesn't matter. However, when the consequences of the decision could really matter, it's a big problem.

"When you're making decisions on your project, or you are part of a decision-making group, you need to understand what's influencing the way you see the world, so you can make 'eyes open' choices."

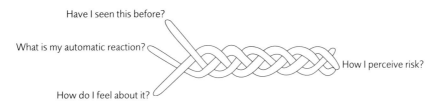

Have I seen this before?

What is my automatic reaction?

How do I feel about it?

How I perceive risk?

Figure 9 The Triple Strand of Influences

Source: Adapted from Murray-Webster and Hillson[18]

This includes understanding, and being able to talk about, what you are feeling in a calm and rational way. You cannot do this unless you have a strong mindful awareness muscle.

Simon, a programme director working in infrastructure, explains how he introduced this idea to his board.

Paralympics and projects: Simon's story

"In the run-up to the Paralympics, I watched an interview with an athlete who is a wheelchair user. She was talking about how she gets severe neck and back pain; how it affects her mind and what she needs to do to prepare herself psychologically before competing.

"Then it occurred to me – there are parallels with working from home. Essentially, we're strapped to our chairs while on Zoom or Teams. She might have got used to being confined like this, but it's alien for us.

"If she wants to be at her best, she knows that she needs to take time to be with herself. Before a big competition, every 45 minutes she spends 20 minutes paying attention to her needs. Her paying attention includes reflecting on how she feels and working out where, and how, she needs to stretch to unravel the knots in her back and her neck. She knows that getting into the right frame of mind takes a combination of mental and physical exercise.

"We're not competing in the Paralympics, but as project leaders and board members we are making major decisions that involve large sums of money and impact people's lives – so it's vital we are in the right frame of mind.

"I started the next programme board meeting by talking about this athlete's mental preparation. I explained that we need to declutter our minds to ensure that we are fully present if we want to weigh up *all* the parameters and data, and ensure we are making intelligent decisions.

"Then, right there in the meeting, I took a risk – I started doing some desktop yoga exercises. I rolled my shoulders and stretched, and invited my chief executive and all the programme board members to join me. And I challenged them all to switch their cameras on.

"Roll forward six months, and we had a big corporate event, which included a state-of-the-nation address from our chief executive. Picture him on screen, live streamed and surrounded by tiles showing over five hundred staff, as well as members of the executive team. It was quite something when he introduced a yoga instructor and invited her to take us all through some yoga moves (cameras on, of course!) to set the scene for clear, mindful thinking.

"On our programme, being mindful and paying attention to how you're feeling is mainstream, now. We routinely press the pause button during a meeting and take time out to get our Thinking brains online. Our contractors and stakeholders are starting to do the same."

I find Simon's story particularly encouraging because he works in infrastructure – a sector that is typically associated with command and control; a sector where you might expect people to dismiss the notion of mindful awareness as 'a bit soft'.

Simon skilfully avoided this by framing mindful awareness as 'doing the mental preparation for quality decision making'. This notion of doing the mental preparation for quality decision making is sometimes described as cognitive readiness.

Quality decisions need cognitive readiness

If you've read the earlier section on mindful awareness with interest, but are concerned that the term 'mindful awareness' won't be well received by those you want to influence, you may prefer to talk about cognitive readiness.

I first encountered this term in the book *Cognitive Readiness in Project Teams*. It describes how the United States Department of Defense asked the question: "How do we ensure our people are able to take the best possible decisions on the battlefield, where they are dealing with rapidly changing environments and inherently risky and emotionally charged situations?"[19]

The answer: individuals and teams have to be 'cognitively ready' – they need the skills and know-how to process vast amounts of information, ranging from the technical to the emotional and social, in real time, and they need the focus, judgement and trust to act on what they find.

There are numerous parallels between the battlefield and complex projects: ambitious objectives, high stakes, the need to cope with frequent, unexpected events and multiple unpredictable players, to name a few.

What does all this mean in practice at a skills level? Take a look at the Cognitive Readiness Framework in Figure 10. It offers an alternative, but complementary, view of what it means to have a strong mindful awareness muscle.

Figure 10 highlights three intelligences: emotional, social and cognitive. In this context, intelligence means 'the ability to understand, recognise and use this type of information to achieve effective or superior performance'. You'll remember, we explored emotional and social intelligence as questions in Figure 6 on page 46. We get to the third intelligence, cognitive (the ability to analyse complex situations and recognise systemic patterns), by using the tools introduced in Part 3.

I'm not fussed whether you talk about cognitive readiness or mindful awareness. What's important is that you see the cross-overs, and that you have a route to enhanced human interaction, teamwork and decision-making, based on an understanding of how the human brain works.

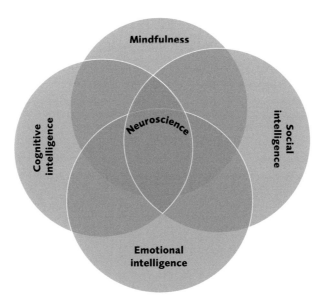

Figure 10 The Cognitive Readiness Framework

Source: Belack et al. [20]

Takeaways

Skills and mindful awareness

- Our ability to succeed in a VUCA world hinges on having:
  - □ the self-awareness to know when your Thinking brain is going offline; and
  - □ the know-how, or self-management, to bring it back online.
- These two skillsets are also the foundation stones for emotional intelligence.
  - □ We can define emotional intelligence as a series of questions, as in Figure 6.
- The ability to recognise when our Thinking brain is going offline and being able to bring it back online is also known as 'being mindful'. The quicker we can recognise when it is going offline and bring it back online – the stronger our mindful awareness muscle.
- When we have a strong mindful awareness muscle, our attention does not get hijacked by memories of the past, or fantasies about the future – we can be truly present.

Echoes from the past – how memory works

- We always behave the way we do for very good reason. Understanding how memory works helps us make sense of behaviour (ours and others').
- We have two types of memory, explicit and implicit.
  - □ Explicit memories include people, facts, objects and events – when we access them, we have a sense of recalling something.
  - □ Implicit memories include images, feelings, habits and the sensory, body-based skills. They can pop into awareness for no apparent reason. When we access them, we don't feel as if we are remembering anything at all.
- We often work too hard at problem solving. Our minds need the mental space that comes with letting things simmer on the back burner, to link up the disparate thoughts and memories that create 'Aha moments'.
- Sometimes our 'mental filing' does not work properly. When this happens our autopilot (neuroception) can get things wrong and make an inaccurate assessment of threat levels – resulting in behaviours that make no sense to an external observer.

- When mental filing goes wrong, we can be left with free-floating, implicit memories that pop up from nowhere and account for our seemingly irrational decisions and behaviour (this mechanism also accounts for the symptoms of PTSD).
- Some things, including moments of intense emotions such as terror and rage, and exposure to high levels of stress over extended periods, make poor mental filing more likely.
- Sometimes we need external assistance to get our mental filing working smoothly for us.

Promoting mental health

- We are all on a continuum of mental health, just as we are with physical health – more, or less, mentally fit and healthy from time to time.
- Our experiences and our environment are primary factors in our mental health every day, far outweighing the impact of heredity or biochemistry.
- Promoting mental health on projects is not about sunk costs or becoming a therapist. It is about securing a ROI (return on investment) of £5 for every £1 spent *and* paying attention to our innate human need for safety, connection and a sense of belonging.

Fantasies of the future

- The brain is an anticipatory machine, constantly scanning and trying to predict what will come next, based on our past experiences. As it does this, it brings up the emotions that accompanied our past experiences and projects them onto our imagined future.
- The trick is to:
  □ recognise this for what it is – fantasy, and an avoidance response in overdrive, and
  □ do something to bring your Thinking brain back online, and your focus back to the present.

Risk assessment, decision making and cognitive readiness

- When the consequences of a decision on your project could really matter, it's vital to understand what's influencing the way you see the world, so that you can make 'eyes-open' choices.

- This means understanding, and being able to talk about, what you are feeling in a calm and rational way.
- You cannot do this unless you have a strong mindful awareness muscle.
- The Cognitive Readiness Framework, shown in Figure 10, offers an alternative, but complementary, view of what it means to have a strong mindful awareness muscle.

References

1 Goleman, D, Boyatzis, R. (2017), *Emotional Intelligence Has 12 Elements. Which Do You Need to Work On?* available at: https://hbr.org/2017/02/emotional-intelligence-has-12-elements-which-do-you-need-to-work-on (accessed 13 July 2021)

2 Williams M, quoted on http://www.mindfulnet.org/index.htm (accessed 15 May 2018)

3 Brown, P, Kingsley, J, & Paterson, S. (2015), *The Fear-free Organisation: Vital Insights from Neuroscience to Transform Your Business Culture*, London: Kogan p72

4 Blake, A (2018) *Your Body is Your Brain*, USA, Trokay Press, p29

5 Brown, P, Kingsley, J, & Paterson, S. (2015), *The Fear-free Organisation: Vital Insights from Neuroscience to Transform Your Business Culture*, London: Kogan p72-75

6 Siegel, D. (2011), *Mindsight: the new science of personal transformation*, New York, Bantam Books p154-157

7 See this video for a summary: The Trauma Foundation (2021), *Trauma and the Nervous System: A Polyvagal Perspective,* available at: https://www.youtube.com/watch?v=ZdIQRxwT1I0. (accessed: 10 November 2021)

8 Leslie, K. (2021), *A Question of Leadership*, London, Bloomsbury, p217

9 Osterweil, C. (2021), How do you manage an invisible workforce? *IT NOW*, March 2021 p50

10 Deloitte (2020), *Mental Health and Employers: Refreshing the Case for Investment*, available at: https://www2.deloitte.com/uk/en/pages/consulting/articles/mental-health-and-employers-refreshing-the-case-for-investment.html?id=uk:2em:3cc:4dcom_share:5awa:6dcom:consulting. (accessed 13 December 2020)

11 Siegel, D. (1999), *The Developing Mind – Toward a Neurobiology of Interpersonal Experience*, New York, Guilford Press, p30

12 Mindful, *Getting Started with Mindfulness*, available at: https://www.mindful. org/meditation/mindfulness-getting-started/(accessed 7 May 2021)

13 Cambridge Dictionary, *Meditation,* available at: https://dictionary. cambridge.org/dictionary/english/meditation (accessed 7 May 2021)

14 Brown, P, Kingsley, J, & Paterson, S. (2015), The Fear-free Organization, London, Philadelphia & New Delhi, Kogan Page. p144

15 Mindful, *Getting Started with Mindfulness*, available at: https://www.mindful. org/meditation/mindfulness-getting-started/(accessed 7 May 2021)

16 Murray-Webster, R, & Winton, E. (2021), *The Disruption Game Plan: New rules for connected thinking on innovation and risk*, Practical Inspiration Publishing

17 Murray-Webster, R, & Winton, E. (2021), *The Disruption Game Plan: New rules for connected thinking on innovation and risk*, Practical Inspiration Publishing

18 Image source: Murray-Webster, R, & Hillson, D. (2007), *Understanding and Managing Risk Attitude* by Routledge, p.93

19 Belack, C, de Filippo, D, de Filippo, I. (2019), *Cognitive Readiness in Project Teams*, New York & Abingdon, Routledge p20

20 Image source: Belack, C, de Filippo, D, de Filippo, I. (2019), *Cognitive Readiness in Project Teams*, New York & Abingdon, Routledge. p27

6

The way we see the world

We've already seen that many things inform the way we see the world. I want to highlight two more factors that are critically important in the project world. They are interrelated. You'll recognise one from the discussion of sources of social threat on page 29 – it's our orientation to certainty and uncertainty. I call the other *'the dance between left and right'*. You'll need to read the next section, 'A brain of two halves', to understand why this dance is so important.

A brain of two halves

I started Part 2 by contrasting the classical view of the brain (which assumed we could identify different parts of the brain, each with a different function), with the view of modern neuroscientists, who see the brain as a complex system that is constantly reconfiguring itself.

Despite knowing that we cannot cut a brain in half to find two hemispheres with different functions, I am going to introduce you to the classical notions of the left and right brain. As I do so, please bear in mind that I am not being literal. When I refer to the left brain, I am talking about the neural networks that give us access to speech and language. When I refer to the right brain, I'm talking about the neural networks that give us access to emotions, physical sensations and whole-body sense.

Iain McGilchrist explains that our survival depends on our ability to pay two kinds of attention to the world around us at once. Picture a cat or dog with its attention locked onto a mouse. Confident and single minded, it has no time or interest in what else might be going on. This narrow focus on a fragment of the bigger picture is left-brain work. It has its uses: "It enables us to grasp and manipulate the world for our own ends." [1]

However, this short-term focus will not guarantee survival. We also need the ability to pay attention to what else might be going on, *at the same time*. This is the work of the right brain – more tentative and less certain than the left, the right brain enables us to see the bigger picture and how we relate to it.

The left and right brain make sense of reality very differently, too. For example, the left specialises in *explaining* with rational sequencing: 'this and then that, and then', whereas the right *describes,* with rich pictures and sensory information.[2].

To understand the significance of this, let's revisit the driving lesson on page 51. What would it look like without the right brain's descriptions?

One Sunday afternoon, a mother was in a car, teaching her daughter to drive. The daughter turned the corner. The mother panicked and told her daughter to pull over. The daughter did so.

We'd be left with a dry explanation, and no felt-sense of what happened.

There are more differences, see Figure 11, which link to how our brains develop.

Consider a baby endeavouring to communicate to its caregivers. Whether cooing and smiling with contentment, or wailing and flailing with frustration, the baby has no words. All its communication is done through gestures, facial expressions, and tonal sounds.

This communication is routed through the right-brain networks. Active at birth, these develop through our first communications, long before the left starts to come on stream.

Remember Figure 1 on page 26. It shows how information flows from the body to the Brainstem to the Feeling brain before it reaches the Thinking brain. This information flow is mostly non-verbal, through the right-brain networks.

Our left-brain networks develop as we acquire language. Language enables us to put words onto things, and to communicate abstract thoughts, logic and conceptual thinking.

These left-brain abilities have been vital in developing the world we live in, and they have a downside. They're becoming more and more dominant in our culture and organisations.

With this trend, and we see it on projects too, we don't routinely pay enough attention to the right-brain worldview, which gives us insight into emotional and social communication and allows us to hold on to multiple possibilities at once.

There are two key messages here.

- The left and right brain networks work together in a complex dance – we need them both.
- We need to actively correct the imbalance if we are to succeed in projects and in life.

Left brain	Right brain
later developing	early developing
linear thinking	holistic
linguistic	non-verbal
logical	raw emotions
literal	whole body sense
loves labels	loves images
loves lists	loves metaphor
loves on/off categories and either/or thinking	loves interconnecting possibilities

Figure 11 The left and right brain

Now, I've two questions for you:

1. Have you spotted the link between implicit memory (page 50) and the right brain networks?
2. Were you tempted to use Figure 11 as a diagnostic?

If your answer to question 2 is yes, let me counsel against it.

Just look what's written in Figure 11. Left-brain networks like on/off categories and either/or thinking. If someone with a strong left-brain dominance hears a right-brain worldview – which is full of interconnecting possibilities – they are likely to dismiss it as 'just plain wrong'.[3]

Don't let your left-brain networks dismiss the potential value of what your right-brain networks bring!

The dance between left and right on projects

Now consider all those formal and informal methods of communication at work. The project plans, the issue logs, the risk registers, and the related conversations over cups of coffee, in virtual meetings and around a meeting room table.

What do you notice about the dance between left and right brain? Are you, your colleagues, sponsors and stakeholders giving both equal airtime in all contexts? Are you comfortable doing so? Do your actions show that you believe it's helpful, legitimate, or even safe to do so?

In my view, left-brain dominance explains a lot of the problems we encounter on projects. Consider our orientation to certainty and uncertainty, for example.

Orientation to certainty and uncertainty

Project 2020

Project 2020 was run by a senior team. Its remit was to restructure a partnership organisation delivering health and social care across the NHS, and central, regional and local government.

Government policy was changing so fast that every time the team got a clear sense of the way forward, there'd be a new policy announcement and the goalposts shifted. For the team, who'd been schooled in traditional project management methods, it was a nightmare.[4]

How could they deliver?

They were desperate for clear parameters, but the steering group were unable to oblige. The environment was moving too fast and, no matter how much they wished otherwise, there was little they could do to influence it.

The Project 2020 team first glimpsed light at the end of the tunnel when, during a team meeting, I offered a label, courtesy of complexity theorists Kurtz and Snowden,[5] to describe their environment. It was un-ordered.

"In un-ordered environments, so much is changing on so many fronts that it seems impossible to keep up, let alone influence the way forward ...

"The way to thrive is to recognise that the lack of order is NOT a matter of poor investigation, inadequate resources or lack of understanding. It is simply a characteristic of a complex system at work. What's more, the lack of order is not necessarily a bad thing, or a problem that can be resolved if someone else would only set their mind to it."

For the 2020 team, this one word, un-ordered, was worth its weight in gold. It validated what, at some level, they had individually come to understand – the lack of order was here to stay, for the foreseeable future at least.

In one way nothing had changed – they still had to deliver.

In another, everything had shifted.

They had permission to acknowledge reality and revise their baseline assumptions. Their usual approach, which aimed to create certainty across the board (and was driven by left-brain dominance), would never pay off, and in this VUCA world there was no point in pretending it would.

This recognition opened the way for a very different approach, which ultimately led to a successful outcome.

My intervention with the Project 2020 team worked on several levels. It introduced a new frame of reference – that of complex systems – to help make sense of the situation they found themselves in. This radically changed the way team members thought about the SCARF domain of certainty.

It created a climate where they could admit that things felt chaotic, without fear of being the only person who thought the project was going off the rails. They saw that the sense of chaos reflected the state of the system; it was not caused by their inability to lead or control. They felt psychologically safe enough to speak about how stressful and difficult things were, without fear of being blamed, punished or rejected for speaking up. With Thinking brains online, they could:

- relax and stop trying to force-fit their project in its entirety to standard tools and methods;
- separate the aspects of the project which were un-ordered from those which were ordered;
- use standard methods where there was order;
- use dialogue and sense-making elsewhere;
- be confident that order would emerge.

This approach has much in common with the one outlined by Mark Phillips[6] as he explores the differences between complexity and risk. He suggests we have choices about how to treat uncertainty. We can choose an orientation towards certainty, or an orientation towards uncertainty. The differences are summarised below.

If your orientation is towards *certainty*	
You fundamentally believe:	▪ All drivers of uncertainty can be identified
	▪ We can estimate their potential impact on outcomes and put plans in place to deal with this
	▪ There may be unknowns and unknown unknowns, but these too can be identified and managed away

If your orientation is towards *uncertainty*	
You fundamentally believe:	▪ The drivers of uncertainty cannot be identified ahead of time
	▪ It's not possible or desirable to plan how best to deal with an unforeseen event before it occurs. Doing so will constrain the project's ability to deliver ambitious results

Figure 12 Is your orientation towards certainty or uncertainty?

Source: Visible Dynamics

When I started working with the Project 2020 team, they fundamentally believed that all drivers of uncertainty could be identified. They were struggling to make their project fit a model that required an orientation to certainty.

They didn't realise they were doing this, and they didn't realise there was an alternative approach – why would they?

Reflecting on this, and my experience of working with others facing similar challenges, the metaphor of the tail wagging the dog springs to mind.

There is a place for traditional risk management, but too often it's the default approach. When setting up and delivering ambitious and complex projects, it's crucial that the key players are comfortable with some things being unknowable. They need an orientation towards uncertainty.

This allows a clear definition of the 'dog', through candid discussion about the unknowns and the flexibility to deal with whatever might arise. With this framework in place, traditional risk management, with its ability to identify and deal with knowable risks, comes into its own.

When we work on complex projects without this over-arching framework, traditional risk management can push stakeholders into conflict, as new and unforeseen challenges appear, especially if they lack the trust and ability to explore perceived risks in depth.

To avoid the risk management tail wagging the dog, we must build environments that are oriented towards uncertainty at the outset. To see how this can be done successfully, look at the story of the UK's Vaccination Taskforce on page 141. Alan's story below illustrates how easy it is to get into hot water if you get this wrong.

The moving go-live date: Alan's story

Alan, a programme director, reflects on his experience of working on a high-profile programme that had already missed one go-live date.

"The media chases headlines. Failure makes a great story; so do rage and fury. Telling the truth and saying, 'we'll go live when it's safe to do so', doesn't capture attention in the same way.

"With all the pressure, we went against our better judgement and, with some misgivings, revised the go-live date to July. But it still wasn't enough.

"When the stakes are this high, decisions go up the food chain. I was hauled in to meet our chief executive. I respect him enormously, but he was clearly frustrated when he asked, 'Why can't you give me a confirmed go-live date?'

"I replied: 'Well, I can. I'm happy to lie if you want me to. But the honest answer is we don't know. This has not been done before, and it's going to take as long as it's going to take.'

"Thankfully, he accepted my answer. I only had the courage to be so direct because I'd spent time thinking about the nature of uncertainty. I'd concluded that it's OK not to know. In fact, when you don't know, the worst thing you can do is to pretend that you do know.

"You can legitimately say: 'This is happening, but it's not our fault; it's not anybody's fault. It's just part of being at the leading edge of something very exciting.' Realising that I could be out and proud about being uncertain was a turning point."

Takeaways

A brain of two halves

- It can be helpful to picture the brain in terms of neural networks (the classicists thought it had two actual halves). Those which give us access to:
  - speech and language (left-brain networks);
  - emotions, physical sensations, and whole-body sense (right-brain networks).
- These networks attend to the world, and make sense of reality, in very different ways. For example, the left focuses on here and now, short term and certain, while the right focuses on the bigger picture and possibilities and is comfortable with uncertainty. Other differences are shown in Figure 11.
- To survive in the world, we need both sets of networks to work together in a complex dance.
- In recent decades we have prioritised a left-brain view of the world.
- We must correct this imbalance to succeed in projects and organisations.

Orientation to certainty and uncertainty

- Sometimes the environment is un-ordered, because so many things are changing on so many fronts that it seems impossible to keep up, let alone influence the way forward ...
- Un-order is NOT a matter of poor investigation, inadequate resources or lack of understanding. It is a characteristic of a complex system at work.

- To succeed in a VUCA world, we must be able to talk explicitly about uncertainty and keep our Thinking brains online as we do so.
- On projects, this ability is a key to creating psychological safety and appropriate governance.

References

1 McGilchrist, I. (2014), Anyone With Half a Brain Can See That! available at: https://www.youtube.com/watch?v=DiPrM0DNI8w. (accessed 2 April 2021)
2 Siegel, D. (2011), Mindsight: the new science of personal transformation, New York, Bantam Books p114–115
3 Siegel, D. (2011), Mindsight: the new science of personal transformation, New York, Bantam Books p109
4 Osterweil, C. (2019), Project Delivery, Uncertainty and Neuroscience, a Leader's Guide to Walking in Fog, Visible Dynamics. p14
5 Kurtz, CF, and Snowden, DJ (2003), The new dynamics of strategy: Sense making in a complex and complicated world, available at: http://alumni.media.mit.edu/~brooks/storybiz/kurtz.pdf (accessed: 1 November 2018)
6 Phillips, M. (June 2014), Defining Complexity for Practitioners PM World Journal, Vol. III, Issue VI, available at http://pmworldjournal.net/article/defining complexity practitioners/(accessed: 1 November 2018)

Part 3. Tools to improve delivery performance

In Part 2 we discovered that we need our Thinking brains online if we are to learn well, collaborate well, be creative and do all the things that are necessary to deliver projects successfully. We also learned that a strong mindful awareness muscle plays a crucial role in helping us do this.

As soon as we recognise that the emotions and behaviour of one person has an impact on the emotions and behaviours of others, we can't get away from the fact that each of us contributes to the situation we find ourselves in.

This was illustrated graphically with the Project Stress Cycle (page 34), which showed how excess stress gets amplified across a project or system. You or I could be Fred in that story, the person responsible for making a VUCA or complex project more VUCA.

It came up again with decision making, when we saw the impact of our cognitive biases and raw, visceral emotions (page 58).

In summary, no matter what our role, if we want our projects to succeed, it's vital that we consider how we are contributing to the situation at a local, team and, on occasion, systemic level through:

- our emotions and behaviours;
- the way we see the world;
- the choices we make.

Part 3 contains a powerful toolkit to help you do this. Its main focus is the application of neuroscience to optimise delivery. However, because some of the tools may surprise you, or seem a bit off the wall, I have included some additional inputs where necessary.

I have tried hard to keep it simple, but this isn't always possible. Interactions between just two people are complex. Scale this up to include the tens, hundreds or even thousands of people involved in delivering a single project, and it can get very messy – there is no point in pretending otherwise!

I've taken the view that I'll serve you best by offering you tools to help you cut through and contain the complexity, peppered with just enough examples to illustrate their application. You'll find more extended case studies in Part 4.

The tools largely answer a series of questions. You'll recognise some of them from Figure 6 on page 46, emotional intelligence as questions.

Neuroscience for project success

We start with Chapter 7, Looking in on yourself, and gaining insight into how you contribute to the situation through:

1) The way you see the world

Fundamentally, this means unpicking the assumptions and structures you, and your organisation, bring. For example,

- Do I/my organisation have an orientation towards certainty or uncertainty?
- What impact does this have on the way I/we think about our projects, decisions and actions?
- Do I/we need to remember to give space to right-brain ways of perceiving the world?

2) Your emotions and behaviour

- How online is my Thinking brain?
- How might I be contributing to the situation through my emotions and behaviour?
- How do I get my Thinking brain more online?

Once you've got insight into yourself and how you're contributing to the situation, you are in a position to move on to Chapter 8, Looking outside yourself. The tools here are based on a second set of questions, which expand the frame and invite you to consider others and the system in which you are operating:

- What can I do to help others get their Thinking brains online?
- What else might be going on in this team/system?
- What tools could help?

Chapters 7 and 8 come with a health warning. You'll be disappointed with the results if you attempt to evaluate the tools through skim reading. *You have to use them if you want to optimise your learning.*
    Go on, I dare you, try them out!

7

Start by looking in on yourself

How am I contributing to the situation through the way I see the world?

In Parts 1 and 2, the themes of complexity and VUCA environments and relationships came up again and again. In my experience, it's important to get beyond the labels and to find ways of unpicking the assumptions and structures we bring.

The tools below, based on Figure 13, will help you to do this by clarifying the complexity.

Clarifying complexity

The framework in Figure 13 combines Eddie Obeng's project typology[1] with Ralph Stacey's work on complexity.[2] It allows us to consider:

- our assumptions about the nature of our project, and
- our orientation towards certainty and uncertainty.

Stacey suggests the two dimensions for considering the nature of complexity shown in Figure 13:

- the degree of divergence of view (about the way forward, processes to be used etc.), and
- the degree of uncertainty about the future.

Both are subjective. I focus primarily on the second.

People working on the same project often have very different views about where to position the project on these two axes – especially when they come from different organisations, different stakeholder groups or even different levels or specialities within the same organisation.

We know from the discussion in Part 2 that perceived social threats, from any of the SCARF domains, have the potential to evoke avoidance emotions and behaviours (remember Fred and the Project Stress Cycle). Unconscious assumptions about certainty inevitably guide every aspect of our work.

Learning to surface and explore our own assumptions about certainty is a crucial skill. Later we'll see how we can use the framework in Figure 13 to surface and explore the assumptions of others.

✎ What kind of project are you dealing with?

Look at Figure 13 and consider two positions. The top right, where there is pressure to deliver even though we are peering into a future we cannot predict (for example, Project 2020), and the bottom left, where we have absolute clarity and clear agreement about the way forward (the terrain of traditional project management processes).

When you are working on a project in the top right, it's like *Walking in Fog*. When Walking in Fog, the best approach is to set out to explore and understand the uncertainty. You make progress by explicitly exploring the terrain, aiming to put stakes in the ground as you gain clarity, and making informed decisions about where to look next to reduce the uncertainty further.

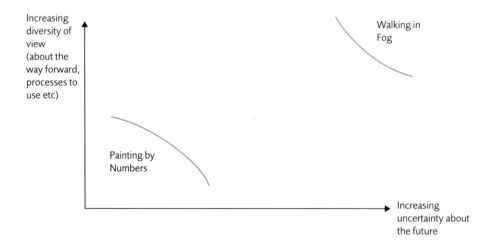

Figure 13 What kind of project are you dealing with?
Source: Visible Dynamics

Working in this way, you move from the top right towards the middle of Figure 13, eventually developing enough experience of the terrain to make realistic risk assessments.

When you reach this point, it's appropriate to adopt more traditional approaches to project planning and risk management – approaches that are akin to *Painting by Numbers*. Essentially, there is sufficient outline of the way forward to make filling in the detail relatively straightforward. The case study about the UK Vaccine Taskforce in Part 4 is a perfect illustration of a project moving from top right to bottom left.

I find Figure 13 particularly helpful because, by using metaphor, it allows us to access knowledge held in the right brain; we all know, or can imagine, what it feels like to be Walking in Fog, and we all know, or can imagine, what it feels like to be a child playing a game like painting by numbers.

Figure 13 is also powerful, because it allows a seamless shift in language from uncertainty to risk without making judgement about which is more appropriate. If you need a reminder, the points below, from *Project Resilience*, clarify the differences.[3]

Risk and uncertainty

- Risks are associated with clarity and predictability – they can be quantified through a rational assessment of how likely, based on past experience, an event is to occur. These assessments are the basis of risk management approaches.
- Uncertainties are assumptions associated with ambiguity and novelty – they are difficult to articulate and define, but this shouldn't prevent you treating them seriously and exploring them carefully. After all, uncertainties that come to pass have a real, and sometimes catastrophic, impact on delivery and outcomes.

Figure 13 provides a language to talk about where we feel most comfortable (our orientation towards certainty/uncertainty). It also provides a language to talk about and, as we'll see later, compare our expectations about the journey ahead.

Project expectations go beyond the rational, left-brain discourse that characterises most project-related conversations (strategies, objectives, activities, risks etc.).

Earlier, we said the human brain is wired for survival; it trusts its own experience above all else. We are constantly comparing the current moment with past experience and making unconscious assumptions about what will happen next. These assumptions drive our thoughts, emotions and behaviours.

They inform what I call our 'inner, personal expectations'. These expectations are the stuff of the right brain. They are determined by how we imagine, and sometimes fear, the project will or might unfold. Figure 14 contrasts business-related expectations with our inner expectations.

The latter rarely figure explicitly in project-related conversations. Yet they have an impact. They contribute to the dynamics and the emotional content, and they determine the tone.

Inner, personal expectations include thoughts and feelings that are hard to admit in public, and sometimes hard to admit to ourselves. They appear in the stories we tell ourselves about what will happen and what has happened – stories that vary, depending on who we are talking to and how safe we feel.

It's easy to dismiss inner, personal expectations as irrational – until we view them through a neuroscience lens. Then it becomes clear that we need to take them seriously.

✂ Exploring preferences

Each of us has a natural preference for different spaces on Figure 13.

I have worked with people who love being in the top right corner and Walking in Fog. They are energised by the constant uncertainty and the relationship-building required to deliver. Put them into stable situations requiring Painting by Numbers and they are like caged birds.

Project expectations	
Business related	**Personal, Inner**
All the things we usually talk about:	*Thoughts and feelings we don't speak about (and often don't admit to ourselves) including:*
■ Business objectives ■ Strategies ■ Systems and processes ■ Plans and risks ■ Finance	■ What we imagine or fear the project will be like ■ Based on: 　■ our past experiences 　■ stories we've heard from others 　■ what's happening right now (in the room, and elsewhere in our lives)

Figure 14 Project expectations

Source: Visible Dynamics

I have worked with others who are most comfortable Painting by Numbers and experience working with uncertainty as stressful.

When you understand how the human brain works, it's clear that no place on the plot is better than another. What's important is the ability to recognise preferences (your own and others') and the implications.

Use Figures 13 and 14 to give insight into your own assumptions and preferences:

- Start by thinking about your own project; where would you place it on Figure 13?
- Consider your own preferences. Where are you most comfortable – Walking in Fog or Painting by Numbers? And what are the implications?
  For example, if it's Painting by Numbers and your project is very foggy, think back to Part 2 – what will this be doing to your Thinking brain?
- Now go to Figure 14. What are your inner personal expectations about the project?
- As you reflect on your answers to these questions, what are the themes, messages and new insights you gain?

Some people find reflecting on these questions leads to big Aha moments. For others, the insights are far more nuanced. Either way, don't dismiss them.

How am I contributing through the stories I tell?

I'm guessing that there are times on your project when somehow, you're stuck. And when we're stuck, we tend to tell ourselves the same stories again and again. What are the stories you tell yourself?

The story might be about what you did, and how it didn't work; what you're going to do, and how that will prevent various scenarios playing out. Or maybe your story conveys a sense of Groundhog Day – every time I try to fix this, the same thing happens.

We explored echoes from the past, and fantasies of the future, in Part 2 – are you caught up in one of these patterns? Or perhaps it's just that now you've stopped for a moment, you have a sense that something, you may not be sure what, is just not quite right. If so, you're not alone!

Repetitive stories like these are signs that your Thinking brain is not completely online. Retelling them doesn't help resolve the situation. The way forward is to get your Thinking brain online, by getting out of your head and becoming really present. One of the most effective ways of doing this is to take a mindful moment.

✎ Mindful moments

In essence, being mindful means knowing what you're experiencing while you're experiencing it.

You may already be skilled at taking a mindful moment. If you are new to the idea, there are numerous techniques, websites, apps and resources to help you.

Two techniques I often use are set out below. I find them particularly helpful because they only take a minute or two (although you can do them for longer), and they lend themselves to so many situations.

Next time your project runs into difficulty, a stakeholder unexpectedly changes their position, or you are disappointed by the conclusions of a review board, STOP, and take a few moments to try Steps A and B below.

Step A

This comprises two brief exercises. You can do them sequentially or just use one of them.

Focus on your breath

- Sit or stand with your back straight but not rigid, and plant your feet squarely on the ground.
- Inhale, breathe deeply and exhale slowly.
- Do this a couple of times and then let your breathing settle into its natural rhythm.
- Give yourself a few moments to be curious about your breath; notice how it enters and leaves your body. Let your attention settle at your nostrils, your chest or stomach – it doesn't matter where. What matters is the act of noticing!
- If your mind wanders, gently tell yourself, 'That's what minds do', and gently bring your attention back to your breath.
- After a minute or two, move on to Three Things or, go to Step B.

Three Things

You can use this as a standalone technique or as an addition to focusing on your breath. Once again, it's about taking a moment to still your thoughts and be curious – this time about the world around you.

- Allow yourself to be quiet and still.
- Let your attention settle on the sounds around you. What can you hear? A bird through the window, children playing, a clock on the wall, the hum of air conditioning? Whatever it is, allow yourself a moment to savour the sound, and then silently name it and move on. What else can you hear? Do this three times.
- Repeat this exercise, using touch. Reach out to touch something, anything: a window; the fabric of your trousers; a tabletop. Whatever it is, allow yourself a moment to savour how it feels to your fingers. Perhaps the window is cool and smooth, while the tabletop is slightly rough and sticky. Silently name it and move on. Do this three times.
- Now go to Step B.

Step B

- Contrast how you are feeling now and how you were feeling before Step A. Notice the difference in your physical sensations and your energy levels. I'm guessing that you'll observe something like, 'I'm feeling calmer, more relaxed, focused or energised'. Or perhaps 'for a moment or two, there's been less internal chatter'.

The difference might be glaringly obvious, or quite subtle. One is not better than the other; any slight shift is a sign that your Thinking brain is a bit more online.

If you didn't notice an immediate difference, don't worry, and don't dismiss these techniques as unhelpful. It could be that something else is going on. For example, you might have underestimated the amount of stress you are carrying. If this is the case, you may need more than a minute or two to discharge it, or perhaps a different, more active exercise will be more appropriate. It's about experimenting and finding out what helps you get out of your head and get your Thinking brain more online – even if it's only for a moment.

Perhaps you're like one of my coachees, Stuart, a senior project manager.

"We did this two-step, mindful moments exercise and things really began to link up. I recognised the difference in my energy levels. After Step B, I felt like I do when I'm absorbed in my hobby – maintaining classic cars.

"Being mindful is not an abstract idea anymore. I really do know what it's like when I have my Thinking brain online. When I'm working on a car, I can tell when my Thinking brain is going offline, so I put down my tools and take a break. I've got to learn to do the same thing at work."

Experimenting with *Mindful moments* and the tools on pages 82–83 helped Stuart to get out of his head, and access information about his state of mind that had previously been below his level of awareness.

Once he had identified his mindful awareness muscle, he could start strengthening it. We'll look at how to do this on page 97.

But first, I want to go back to the question, 'how am I contributing to the situation?', and offer you two techniques that will enable you to access more of the non-verbal knowledge that's held in your right brain and was set out in Figure 11 on page 69:

- Getting it onto a page;
- Listening to your body.

Getting it onto a page – metaphor and imagery

This technique takes 10–20 minutes and is based on a single question. All you need do is follow the instructions below and remember what I said earlier: reading about tools will not work – you have to try them out!

Choose a project challenge you are facing; perhaps it's a story you constantly revisit.

A. Get a blank piece of paper and a pen or pencil, then read the instructions through to the end of step E.
B. Do a mindful moment exercise to clear your head (page 82).
C. Now imagine you're sitting with a friend in a café or bar. They've realised you want to talk about something important. Picture them asking you the wonderful open question: 'What's it like?'

Your job is to come up with an image or metaphor to give them a flavour of 'What it's like'. They're after an impression, so don't get hung up on accuracy. What's the first thing that comes into your head?

If the idea of an image or metaphor makes your mind go blank, here are some suggestions and examples for you:

- Something from nature: the oceans, animals, birds, planets, landscape, fog, sunshine, a fine spring day ...
- A cartoon character, an advert, a TV programme, film;
- School, sports, family, kitchen, music, ... it really doesn't matter.

There are no rights and no wrongs. When I ask this question in my coaching, I've had answers as varied as: 'I'm like the Road Runner caught between my programme manager and stakeholders'; 'They're like planets in a different galaxy'; 'I'm steamrollered by them' ...

D. Now take one or two minutes, no longer, to make a scrappy image of your metaphor on the page. This is about getting 'what it's like' out of your head and onto the page. There's no point in trying to make it look realistic; just dump it there. Whatever you come up with, whether it's three big blobs of ink, stick people, or an elephant that looks more like an octopus with six legs – it will be good enough! Getting it out of your head and onto a page is the only thing that matters.
The aim is to have something that you can look at and play around with for a few minutes.

So please suspend any judgements about your artistic abilities. Your image is *not meant to be realist*ic – you can stick it in the bin later if you want to.

E. Now look at your image, what does it tell you about the situation?

My Road Runner coachee, Sarah, laughed as she responded: "I'm just running around trying to please them all – and not adding much value."

F. Now's the time to play with a few questions and experiment to find out how you can use the image to get new insights. Questions that could help include:
- How can you change your image to improve the situation a little? What could you add? What could you take away? (Go on, cross it out.)
- What else could you do to it? Zoom in on detail, Zoom out ... or?
- What else? (It doesn't matter how whacky the idea. One coachee's image was a stick man leaning on a crutch. This question prompted him to turn the crutch into a magic wand ... it worked for him!)

- If your image involves several stakeholders, would they all recognise the situation? How might it need tweaking to accommodate each of their points of view?

Sarah shared her image with her team and was delighted with its reception (much merriment and a huge sigh of recognition). She then plucked up the courage to take it to her programme manager. Using the metaphor allowed her to put the tricky right-brain stuff on the table. It was a real breakthrough and led to their first proper conversation about how they could work together more effectively.

G. Who else can you share your image with to help you develop it, or to test your thoughts? 'Am I the only one who thinks/feels this?'

Here are two more illustrations of how I've used *Getting it onto a page* to help people resolve challenges that involve difficult emotions and behaviours at a more systemic level.

Indiana Jones – George's story

A programme manager, George, explained his struggle in a phone call in October.

"My organisation has contracted a delivery agent, (DA), to let the supplier contracts. DA are responsible for making sure we get what we need – and they're not. We've a milestone approaching. The supplier needs to be demonstrating that the kit they've designed passes our tests. They're telling me, 'It's in hand' – I don't believe it! The contractual arrangements mean it's completely out of my control and DA are just sitting back."

We spoke again in January. George reported: "Things have improved, but it's very tenuous. The supplier has appointed a new project manager who is driving for June dates. They're throwing everything at it and are still two to three months behind.

"The testing in December was unimpressive. It was done internally, and that's never good for software system integration. But at least DA have acted, so the supplier is feeling the risk of significant liquidated damages. The supplier has started working with us to come up with a coherent joint narrative on what needs to happen to get a realistic evaluation plan.

"The plan needs to cram everything into six weeks, but the schedule still isn't believable. How do I approach the next three to six months, and next week's governance meeting with our SRO?"

As I listened, I was struck by the number of references to technical detail, and the unspoken undercurrent of frustration and powerlessness.

Figure 11 on page 69 explored how the left and right brain make sense of the world differently, and led to the conclusion that we operate at our best when they work together in a complex dance.

George's description of what was going on was left-brain dominant. I wanted him to complement this by accessing his right brain's worldview and insights into the emotional and social communication, so I took him through Steps A-G of *Getting it onto a page*.

I asked: "What's it like?' and followed this with an invitation. "Take a moment or two to come up with an image or a metaphor, something that will allow you to picture what's going on. You could even try drawing it."

A pause, then George started speaking again. I could hear the rustle of pen on paper down the phone line as he spoke. You can see my scrappy version of what he was saying in Figure 15.

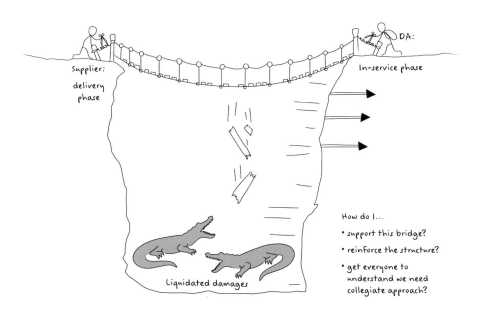

Figure 15 The rope bridge

"We should have had a suspension bridge. But because of the way the contracts have been set up, we have a fragile rope bridge. It's like that scene in the Indiana Jones movie – the rope is fraying.

"When things were at their worst, it was as if the supplier and DA were trying to cut the rope. DA's commercial people are moving to the right – they see maintaining principles as more important than seeing the programme succeed. They don't appreciate there's no benefit in hitting the supplier with liquidated damages."

Remember Steps F and G: once you've got an image or metaphor, the trick is to use it to help you explore what might be happening.

I asked George: "Now we've got a picture, how can we use it to resolve the situation? What questions does it raise?"

The answers came fluently:

- "How can I reinforce the rope and get more support for the bridge?
- "How can I get everybody to understand we need a collegiate approach?
- "If we can have an honest conversation about where we are, it will fix the left-hand side in place. But the supplier and DA are so defensive, how do I start an honest conversation?"

Defensiveness is a sign that your Thinking brain is offline, so when you spot it in someone else, a key question must be: how do I get their Thinking brain more online?

One emotion, surprise or startle, has a particular role in changing attitudes and behaviours. It seems to allow the brain to pause, and in that moment, it creates the possibility for change.[4]

Knowing this, I asked George: "How could you use your image to approach this conversation in a totally different way, one that would be surprising and create new possibilities?"

Three months later, George told me what had happened: "I used my drawing. The supplier has finally acknowledged that they can't make the dates, and things are moving in the right direction. Our gateway review is in two weeks and I'm feeling relaxed about it."

Speaking about difficult emotions: coaching through Covid's story

The second example relates to Coaching through Covid (CtC), a service that I was involved in setting up in the UK in the early days of the pandemic.

CtC's purpose was to support frontline health care staff through the provision of high-quality, pro-bono coaching. The coaching would resource them and increase their resilience at a time when infection rates were spiralling, treatments unknown and hospitals were almost overwhelmed.

The CtC team noted that the Government and media often spoke about 'our NHS angels'. We were concerned: what was it like to be one of these angels, carrying the burden of the nation's hope for survival?

How could we attend to their unspoken, personal stories and expectations, as well as all the left-brain, project-related stuff that always gets airtime?

Figure 16 is based on a sketch I did to capture the reality of life on the frontline. We were asking these 'NHS angels' to walk on water. The virus was tearing through everything they knew like a tornado, and no one was acknowledging what it was like to be wearing a mask.

When we shared it with healthcare workers we were told: "You've captured something I couldn't put into words – it's visceral and cathartic. It gives me permission to speak about things I dared not raise before."

Figure 16 Life on the frontline

What does Life on the Frontline evoke in you?

- Spend a few moments looking at the image.
  - What catches your eye?
  - What impact, if any, does it have at a deeper level?
- Notice any feelings, physical sensations or even memories, (perhaps of the early days of the pandemic, or something totally unrelated to it) that arise.
  - What sense do you make of them?
- Take a mindful moment if you need to.

When you are ready, consider this question:

If you knew you didn't have to worry about your own artistic abilities, because you could always cobble something together using other people's images, photos and paintings from the internet, what thorny challenge might imagery and metaphor help you address?

How am I contributing through my emotions and behaviour?

In the previous section we looked at how metaphor and imagery can help us access non-verbal, right-brain knowledge. We also touched on the feelings and emotions that they can evoke. Let's take this exploration a step further.

I introduced the notion of neuroception (the process of the brain and nervous system working together on autopilot and outside of conscious awareness, to continually assess threat levels and make judgements about what is safe and what is not) on page 27. Stephen Porges, who came up with the term, observed that, while we are not usually aware of the actual cues that trigger it, we can learn to be more aware of the physiological shifts that result.

This section aims to do just that because, as we've seen on previous pages, our physical sensations, emotions, thoughts, memories and actions are inextricably linked, even if many of us have been taught the opposite.

Does that sound far-fetched? Have you ever had butterflies and a dry mouth, ahead of a presentation, for example? What do you do with those sensations – set your jaw, grit your teeth and try to override them? Maybe it worked for you, and maybe it didn't.

Feelings we try to suppress often leak out anyway. Others pick them up through the same process, neuroception. For example, Fred on page 34 may repeatedly tell himself and everyone else that 'everything is under control', and not realise that his body is conveying the opposite.

As a result, his team members and stakeholders are unconvinced – their neuroception picks up (albeit at an unconscious level) his underlying anxiety from the tone of his voice, and the way his eyes dart from side to side as he speaks.

In other words, your body talks and it has an impact.

Your body talks

As you read this, I'm half expecting you to be nodding your head and thinking, 'Self-awareness, body language – I know about that. The best way to develop self-awareness is to get some feedback from others'.

And you're right – you could select some key team members, stakeholders or colleagues and ask them how they experience you. Or, if you're not feeling quite so brave, you could wait for a formal feedback or review meeting.

Getting feedback from others is part of the answer. But there's something else that is even more important.

If your body talks, it's important you develop the skills to listen to it by noticing its tiny shifts and changes. Doing so gives you immense power. Wouldn't it be helpful if, in a meeting, you could put a finger on the source of that queasy feeling that tells you 'this just doesn't feel right', and confidently explain your reasoning rather than bite your tongue?

The moment when you spot your heart is sinking, your chest tightening, or your feet have gone jittery is like gold dust – as long as you recognise it as a legitimate source of information and know what to do with it.

Use this information well (I'll show you how in *Listening to your body*, page 94), and you'll be able to judge how online or offline your Thinking brain is, press the pause button and develop an ability to bring your Thinking brain more online when you need to, as Sanjiv, a project manager based in India, will attest.

A prisoner of technology: Sanjiv's story

Sanjiv was on an audio call, telling me about his recent 360 feedback. "It says I'm not listening enough ... When I hear something I disagree with, I can't help myself – I speak from the heart, and it's causing me problems. The other day I got into an argument with a key stakeholder in the USA."

As I listened, I noticed how fast he was talking, the slightly breathy tone of his voice and the impact of this combination on me. Despite being thousands of miles away in the UK, my heart rate was beginning to go up – a sure sign of neuroception at work – and we weren't even in the same room!

I asked a straightforward, if surprising, question. "Sanjiv, can you bring your attention to your body. Tell me what you notice. It could be anything, how fast your heart is beating, a slight knot in your stomach, a temperature difference, something about your breath, a tension or lightness ... or maybe you notice something entirely different ... And it doesn't have to be big with flashing lights; it could be quite subtle – I just want you to be curious."

Sanjiv thought for a moment and then replied: "There's a bit of tension in my shoulders and neck. Now I'm noticing, my heart rate is a little fast, and my chest is a bit tight as well.'

That was it, the gold dust! We had something to work with. We went on to investigate how he could use this information (see page 95 for the stepped process we used. You'll see, it builds on *Mindful moments*, metaphor and imagery).

I encouraged Sanjiv to explore how he could release some of the tension through movement. I wanted us to discover what worked for him – was it stretching, standing up, shaking his limbs, mindful breathing ... What could he do to shift the tightness?

And when he'd shifted it, what was that like? What were the physical sensations he noticed, and how did it change his energy levels, and his emotional state?

As we explored what was going on, Sanjiv mentioned that he'd started our meeting like all his other meetings. He'd been sitting down with his laptop on a low table. Now he was standing, he'd stretched and taken a few deep breaths, he felt entirely different. He had more energy and felt relaxed in his chest and shoulders.

I told him I could hear it – the quality of his voice had changed too. With more breath it was less staccato and easier to listen to. As he slowed down, I had more time to process what he was saying. In fact, I was able to relax too.

We joked that he'd been a prisoner of technology, and finished the session with a discussion of how he could use this experience to build his mindful awareness muscle.

Two months later we spoke again. Sanjiv told me about his huge strides. He now used a headset and he'd moved his laptop so he could be upright when making calls. This helped him relax. Sometimes, when he wanted his thoughts to flow even more freely, he walked around.

There were still times when things did not go as he wanted and he suspected that his Thinking brain was going offline. When this happened, he'd discovered that it helped to put his hand on his chest as he spoke. This small movement reminded him to consciously deepen his breathing, slow his speech and bring his Thinking brain further online.

What can we learn from this story?

Sanjiv recognised the feedback that he wasn't listening, and he had a level of self-awareness – he knew certain situations triggered unhelpful behaviours. But that wasn't enough. He needed knowledge about how his brain works, and the ability to link his physical sensations to his energy levels, emotions and thought patterns, before he could experiment and work out how to make a lasting change.

I don't know about you, but until I started learning about how the brain works, I went through life paying very little attention to my body. In fact, I'm not sure it's exaggerating to say I didn't really know I had one (unless I happened to twist my ankle or have a headache)!

Sanjiv was no different. Before our conversation he had no idea that he was a prisoner of technology or that his body was a source of information. I'm not being critical – few of us do. Nobody tells us at school, or anywhere else, that the body is a source of information.

This information has a name – somatic intelligence. Somatic intelligence is the underpinning of emotional and social intelligence.[5]

All forms of intelligence come with a health warning. If you are a whizz at numbers, you may add up a column of figures in your head, but you still know to check for errors – it's easy to drop a zero. Somatic intelligence is no different. The body is a legitimate source of information – however, legitimate is not always accurate. We might detect risk where there isn't any, or cues of safety when it's not safe.

But that's not a reason to ignore what our body is telling us. As with the column of figures, we may need to double check and validate our hunches. We can do this by asking a simple question such as, 'Am I the only one feeling a bit anxious?'

In summary, listening to your body is key to developing your mindful awareness muscle, because *the ebbs and flows of physical sensations, moods, thoughts and emotions dictate your actions*. And crucially, as you become more aware of them, like Sanjiv, you become better able to self-regulate and you discover you have choices about how to respond.

✑ Listening to your body

My aim here is to develop your ability to listen to your body, so that you become more familiar with your feelings and physical sensations. Following the steps below will increase your familiarity and develop your mindful awareness muscle. However, developing any muscle relies on repetitions, so you need to do Parts A and B:

A. Listening to your body to recognise when your Thinking brain is online and offline;
B. Building the muscle over time.

Before you get started, please read from the tips below on taking care of yourself right through to the end of 'your body budget' on page 98.

Taking care of yourself

If at any point you feel things are too uncomfortable, then please STOP, and do something that will help you find equilibrium. This might mean taking a mindful moment (page 82), or engaging in another activity that *you know you find calming*. Consider what you might turn to *before* starting Part A.

If you choose to stop, please don't equate this with failure. It's quite the opposite! The act of stopping is a sign that you are learning to regulate yourself better. Explore the fact that you *knew to stop* at a later date, by reflecting on these two questions:

- How did I know to stop this exercise?
- What does my answer to that question tell me about learning to listen to my body?

Now we're ready.

Part A.
Step 1. Recognising how it feels when your Thinking brain is offline

Think of a situation that repeatedly takes your Thinking brain offline. This exercise works best when you choose something that you find quite tricky, but not so tricky that it's completely dysregulating.

Think back to last time it happened. Picture your surroundings and who else was there (in person, virtually or even by email). What was going on? Who (including you), was saying and doing what?

As you start to recall the situation, bring your attention internally.

■ How are you feeling?
■ What are your energy levels like?
■ What physical sensations, no matter how subtle, do you notice? Where do you notice them? What's happening to your breath and your heart rate, your limbs and/or your torso?
■ Be really curious.
■ If it feels safe, you might want to experiment to see if you can amplify and exaggerate these feelings and sensations. For example, if you notice tension in your jaw, you might want to clench it tighter; if you shoulders are rounded you might want to round them more ... you get the idea.
■ Now, just as we did in Step D of *Getting it onto a page* (page 84), imagine you're with a friend you really trust, and they've just asked you that wonderful open question, 'What's it like?'.

Some people can answer this question very quickly; others are not so familiar at describing their feelings and physical sensations.

If this is you, please don't get impatient or self-critical. Instead, remind yourself that you are aiming to build your mindful awareness muscle and, just like me in the Pilates class on page 48, you may need some help in discovering you have one. Then take a look at Appendix C, which includes words to help name feelings and physical sensations.

■ As soon as you've come up with something that gives a flavour of what it's like, scribble it down as a scrappy image or a few words. We're not after accuracy or art, here – just something that means something to you.

Step 2. Recognising how it feels when your Thinking brain is online

■ Take a moment to recall the feelings and physical sensations from Step 1 as vividly as possible.
■ Now move, and do whatever you have to do to shed them.

As with Sanjiv, this might be stretching, standing up, shaking your limbs, mindful breathing and/or doing the Three Things grounding exercise on page 83.

Experiment to discover what works for you.

- When you've done this, allow yourself a few moments to notice the feelings and physical sensations you are experiencing, no matter how subtle. Take a forensic interest in them, just as you did in Step 1.
- See if you can do anything to exaggerate and amplify them.
- Next, imagine describing 'What it's like' to a trusted friend, and scribble down whatever comes into your head as a scrappy image or a few words.

Step 3. Developing a scale

- Take your two scrappy images, or sets of words, and link them up with a line.
- We are going to use this line as a scale from 1 to 10. One end represents when your Thinking brain is completely offline, and the other end represents when it's completely online.

If you're not sure what I mean, use Figure 17 for inspiration – it's a compilation of scrappy images, metaphors and words from conversations with different coachees. Don't worry about artistic merits. All you need is something that is meaningful to you.

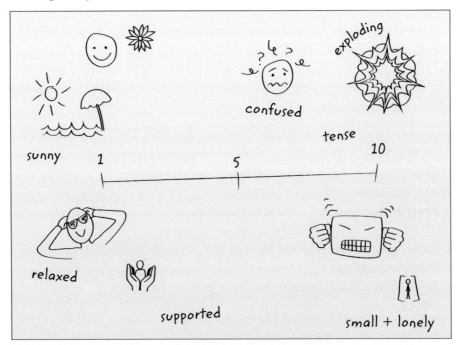

Figure 17 Using images and words to develop a scale

You can use this scale as a tool to judge, at any moment during the day, 'how online or offline is my Thinking brain?'

Part B. Building your mindful awareness muscle

- Get yourself a journal, or use your calendar or a sheet of A3 paper – or whatever will work for you as a log.
- Check in with yourself at least once, and ideally several times, a day. Ask yourself: Where am I on the scale? What do I have to do to get my Thinking brain more online? Maybe it's one of the mindful moment exercises, having a stretch, going for a walk, moving into a different room, stroking your dog or cat, playing with the kids for five minutes, getting a glass of water or …
- Experiment and be curious about the results. What helps shift you in the right direction? What gets in the way? What are the patterns?
- Don't beat yourself up if you miss a day, or your Thinking brain goes offline for a while.
- Remember it's about repetitions to build new neural pathways.

If this all sounds too far-fetched, or like hard work, Donna's story might inspire you to give it a try.

Overcoming the jitters: Donna's story

Donna, a programme lead working in Government, describes what happened.

"I enjoy a high-adrenaline lifestyle – wild swimming, running up mountains, challenging people, challenging situations. I'd moved to a new organisation in a very different role and that, combined with the pandemic and the move to 100 per cent virtual working, knocked my confidence.

"I hated my voice in video meetings; I sounded so uncomfortable – like a nervous schoolgirl. I wanted gravitas and to come across as a person who could inspire trust because they had the situation under control.

"I used to think that I went into those meetings with the nervous energy and excitement I get before a wild swim. But when I slowed down and learned to do the scaling exercise, and contrasted how I felt before and after a mindful moment, I realised something else was going on.

"There's only one way to describe what was happening in my body: I had the jitters. It was nothing like the nervous energy I get before a swim. My toes and feet were moving all over the place under the desk, and my schoolgirl voice was coming from tension in my chest and a shortness of breath. When I did the scaling, I realised that a bit of me was panicking, 'What am I going to face? What am I going to face?' – just like I did when I was a kid, and I was terrified there was a bogeyman hiding behind the door.

"I see it very differently now – something about the meetings triggered me back in time and set off an old fight-or-flight reaction. Once that was in full flow, my brain dredged up all kinds of stuff that fed a negative cycle to justify the way I was feeling.

"As soon as I learned to go, 'Hang on a second, where's that coming from?' I started to break the cycle. I now know to press the pause button, ground myself and get my Thinking brain online, even if it means arriving at an important meeting a couple of minutes late."

Before leaving *Listening to your body*, I want to expand on an idea I touched on earlier, on page 25 – your body budget.

Your body budget

Lisa Feldman Barrett coined the term 'body budget' to draw a parallel between managing financial budgets and managing our body's internal resources. On projects we use budgets to track deposits, investments and withdrawals, and we move money between budget lines to ensure our overall budget stays in balance.

Our brain has circuitry that essentially does the same thing. It deals in different resources – oxygen and food, for example – but the aim is similar: to keep our body budget in balance. Doing this requires it to make constant predictions about your heart rate, breathing, blood pressure, temperature, hormones, metabolism and so on, and to ensure that each is calibrated to your body's actual needs.

She goes on to warn us: "If your body budget gets out of whack, then you're going to feel crappy no matter what self-help tips [or exercises in this book] you follow ... and modern culture [and projects] are unfortunately engineered to screw up your body budget."[6]

We've spoken a lot about dealing with stress and complexity and keeping our Thinking brains online. These daily activities all require us to make withdrawals from our body budgets. Feldman Barrett reminds us we need to make deposits too – there's no substitute for doing the basics, such as getting enough sleep, eating well, ensuring we are well hydrated, connecting with others and getting enough exercise.

Takeaways

- We contribute to the situations we find ourselves in through the way we see the world. Key aspects of this include:
  - □ our orientation towards certainty and uncertainty;
  - □ the stories we tell;
  - □ our emotions and behaviours.

Clarifying how you contribute to the situation through your orientation to certainty and uncertainty

- Clarify your assumptions about the nature of the project you're working on. How do you see it? As: Walking in Fog, Painting by Numbers, or something in between? (See Figure 13.)
- Understand the difference between risk and uncertainty
  - □ risks are associated with clarity and predictability. Based on experience, they can be quantified.
  - □ uncertainties are assumptions associated with ambiguity and novelty. They are difficult to articulate and define, yet important to surface and explore.
- Be clear about your preferences; are you more comfortable Walking in Fog, Painting by Numbers, or something in between?
- We all have unspoken, personal expectations about the projects we work on (Figure 14), but typically it's only business-related expectations that get airtime. We need to learn to surface and talk about our inner, personal expectations too.

Clarifying how you contribute to the situation through the stories you tell

- The stories you tell about your project will have an impact on how it unfolds.
  - □ Repetitive stories can be a sign that your Thinking brain is not completely online.
- Taking a *Mindful moment* can help you be more present by bringing your Thinking brain more online.
- When you are more present, you have more choice about the stories you tell.

- Techniques such as, *Getting it onto the page*, with its images and metaphors, will help you:
  - □ access non-verbal, right-brain knowledge;
  - □ clarify how you, and others, see the world;
  - □ make it possible to talk about emotions and inner expectations, in a matter-of-fact and non-threatening way;
  - □ unstick previously stuck situations.

Clarifying how you contribute to the situation through your emotions and behaviour

- Our physical sensations, thoughts, memories, and actions are inextricably linked.
- Feelings we try to suppress leak out anyway – others pick them up through neuroception.
- Your body talks and it has an impact.
  - □ It's important to develop the skills to listen to your body by noticing its tiny shifts and changes.
  - □ When we notice these shifts, we gain access to 'somatic' intelligence.
  - □ Somatic intelligence is the underpinning of emotional and social intelligence.
- Learning to listen to your body is key to developing your mindful awareness muscle. As you become more aware of the ebbs and flows of physical sensations, moods, thoughts and emotions, you become better able to self-regulate, and you discover you have choices about how to respond.
- The exercise, *Listening to your body*, can help you develop your mindful awareness muscle. As with any muscle, if you want to build strength, you need to do repetitions.

Your body budget

- Our brain has circuitry to 'budget' the resources used in daily life, oxygen and food, for example. As with a financial budget, we need to keep our body budget in balance.
- Daily activities such as dealing with stress and complexity require us to make withdrawals from our body budgets. It's vitally important that we prioritise making deposits too.

References

1 Obeng, E. (1994), *All Change! The Project Leader's Secret Handbook*, London: Pitman p98–99

2 Stacey, RD. (2002), *Strategic management and organisational dynamics: the challenge of complexity*. 3rd ed. Harlow: Prentice Hall

3 Kutsch, E, Hall, M, & Turner, N. (2015), *Project Resilience: The Art of Noticing, Interpreting, Preparing, Containing and Recovering*, London: Gower p7–10

4 Swart, T, Chisholm, K, and Brown, P. (2015), *Neuroscience for Leadership: harnessing the brain gain advantage*, New York and London: Palgrave Macmillan p120

5 Blake, A. (2018), *Your Body is Your Brain*, Trokay Press, USA, p66

6 Feldman Barrett, L. (2018), *How Emotions are Made: The Secret Life of the Brain*, London, Pan Books p176

8

Looking outside yourself: bringing others' Thinking brains online

I've introduced a number of ways to bring your Thinking brain online, come into the present and identify how you are contributing to the situation. When you can do this, you'll be well placed to look outside yourself and:

- recognise when others' Thinking brains are offline;
- make informed choices about the behaviours and interventions required to bring them back online;
- see systemic patterns: for example, how psychologically safe is it? What's the dominant orientation, certainty, or uncertainty? How is stress playing out across the system?
- take a view on if, and how, to intervene.

With so many things to consider, I cannot hope to cover them all from every angle. Instead, I have elected to introduce the approaches I find particularly powerful which build on the themes we've already touched on.

Exploring complexity with others

⚘ What are we dealing with?

You'll recognise the graph in Figure 18 from earlier. Here we are using it as a tool to surface and explore the assumptions of others.

Simply explain the axes, and the terms Painting by Numbers and Walking in Fog, then:

- Ask: 'Where do you see this project?' (Invite them to put an X on the graph.)
- Ask: 'What makes you place it there?'

- Be really curious about the replies. 'What is clear? What is foggy? What do they need to see to make it less foggy?
- Where is there common ground you can build from?
- Where are the differences? What needs to happen to reduce the differences?

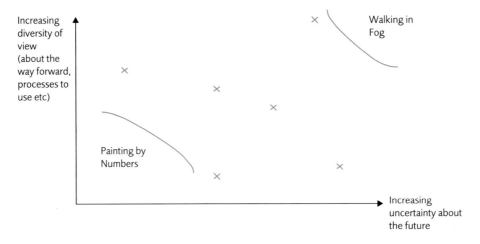

Figure 18 Exploring complexity with others

Enquiring in this way helps to create the psychological safety to enable all involved in project delivery to contextualise and better understand the challenges. It also allows you to value the contribution and experience of those with an orientation towards certainty, while opening a space that makes it possible for them to tolerate discussion about uncertainty, and vice versa.

As you drill down, you'll uncover, possibly for the first time, the aspects of the project that each of you finds particularly ambiguous and worrisome. Together you'll be able to develop focused strategies for dealing with the 'what' of uncertainty. You also need to consider the 'how'.

✎ How can we best work together?

You can also use this graph to explore preferences and how you can best work together. Start with a simple question:

- Where on Figure 18 are you most comfortable operating – Painting by Numbers or Walking in Fog? (Invite them to put an X on the graph.)

You then have the option of probing further, just as we did on page 80. I'd counsel against asking directly about their inner personal expectations. A more elegant of way of finding out about these is to ask: What are your hopes and fears?

Depending on the situation, these opening questions may lead you to the detail. For example, imagine you're speaking to a new team member. You've agreed the project is foggy, and they've told you they find uncertainty difficult to handle. It might help to explore:

- What's likely to take your Thinking brain offline?
- How can you help me spot when this is happening?
- What do we need to put in place to help you keep your Thinking brain online?

Walking in Fog: Leonie's story

Leonie, a programme director, explains how these tools supported her work on a high-profile, multi-faceted programme: "I'd been reflecting on my approach to leadership; people take their cues from you as a leader in formal and informal settings. I can be quite emotional, so I had to find ways of moderating that, and learn to be very careful about who I spoke to when I was feeling pressured.

"The notion of Walking in Fog was so important. I couldn't see past one particular milestone; it was massively foggy and made me very anxious. I spoke about it to my deputy, who is hugely practical. His reply, 'I can figure that out for you', took the pressure off. Taking time to reflect on how I felt, and choosing who to share my nervousness with, was crucial.

"We got through those times because we could rely on each other. I wasn't alone, wandering about in the fog; there was a group of us. Yes, I was leading this particular venture, but others were there to support me and contribute to moving things forward. They didn't expect me to have all the answers (even if at times I thought I should). However, they did expect me to have a sense of which direction to go."

She went on to reflect on how her understanding of stress evolved over time, and how the Stress Cycle had helped. "I came to understand that stress is contagious. If I am stressed, other people are stressed as well. A lot of the time I was dealing with professionals who know how to put on a good front. But underneath, they are human too. I learned to give them the space to be stressed – this meant not reacting if they were a bit sharp or short with me.

"We spoke about this explicitly in the project team. No matter how much stress we were under, others at the frontline were under far more. We needed to cut them a bit of a slack. Rather than taking things personally, it became, 'they're having a difficult time'.

"Using this information by reminding our SRO to acknowledge it, and framing things carefully by saying, 'We're not blaming you, we know this is hard, we know you are doing everything you can', in certain meeting situations made a massive difference.

"This awareness of how, as a group, we were interacting with others who were under pressure, and encouraging my team to be kind so that we didn't do anything to make things worse was a lesson that will stay with me for life."

Using the Stress Cycle

Leonie's story shows one way of using the Stress Cycle; there are many more. Here are another two examples, one from IT and a second from construction.

✍ Influencing upwards: Suzanne's story

Suzanne worked as a senior IT project manager. She had picked up responsibility for a team of 30 and delivery of an urgent IT system by the end of the calendar year. Management had recognised the scale of the challenge and agreed she could recruit 10 more developers.

The additional resources were welcome, but recruitment was taking time and Suzanne was coming under increasing pressure to commit to a delivery schedule that didn't seem realistic. She needed headspace to work out what was required.

Suzanne used the Project Stress Cycle to put her case to her programme director. The programme director was defensive at first, but then saw the systemic pattern, and realised that he was caught up in a similar dynamic. As stakeholders were becoming more anxious about delivery, everyone, including himself and the project's sponsor, was being asked for additional information. Responding to this stream of requests was distracting them all from the work itself. With the dynamic visible, he supported Suzanne in negotiating for what was needed.

Tip: When using the Project Stress Cycle as a tool, it can be helpful to ask 'What part(s) of it resonate?' and highlight the answers, as in Figure 19.

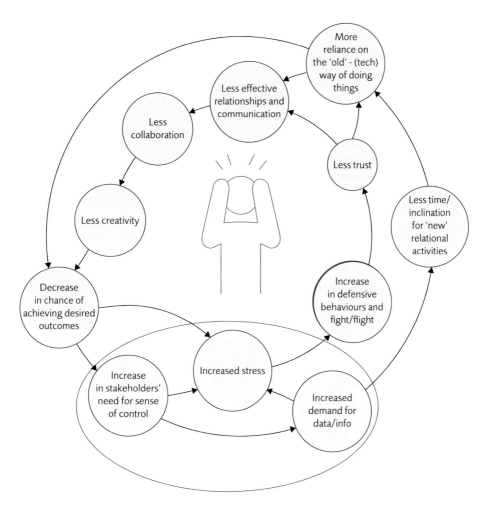

Figure 19 Using the Project Stress Cycle as a tool

✎ Safety moments at project and programme boards: Dan's story

Safety is a massive requirement in infrastructure projects, so team meetings, project and programme boards often start with a safety moment.

Dan describes how it works on his project. "Safety moments can focus on operational staff, delivery staff or even the public. Typically, we use them to bring safety stats and concerns about safety to life by telling a personal story or sharing an insight. This is followed by a challenge. Essentially, you're saying: "This is what I've done, and this is what the team has done. You, board (or team) members, are key influencers – what are you going to do differently?'

"On occasion I've said, 'We've a problem with safety – I think this is happening', and I've put up a slide of the Stress Cycle. This has kicked off a discussion about how to recognise the signs of stress, and how to communicate differently.

"It hasn't stopped there. On more than one occasion, I've done this at a board meeting (and we have lots of them with different stakeholders attending), and I've got a call immediately afterwards from a senior manager. They've then told me that they were having a similar problem and have asked for a copy of the slide.

"Typically, they'd identified the behaviours within their own teams, but they hadn't known how to explain it. If they couldn't explain it, how could they find a solution? The slide enables them to do both. It allows the people who are suffering, in the middle of the diagram, to understand the repercussions of their behaviour – on them personally, and on the wider team, without judgement. It also highlights the impact on interconnections across the whole project."

This mention of interconnections brings us to tools for promoting a sense of connection (the R, relatedness, in the SCARF framework).

Promoting connection

Here I'm going to introduce two tools, Taking 10 and The Check-in. Let's start with Taking 10.

🔧 Taking 10

Mental health advocate Anne Archer explains: "Taking 10 means taking 10 minutes on a regular basis to talk to someone about how things are going. It's NOT about tasks or deadlines. It's a tool that focuses on you, the person and what's going on for you at work and at home. It's about how you are feeling.[1]

"When you get into the habit of regularly Taking 10 at an individual level and at team level, it becomes a normal part of business.

"It is a great way of countering the feelings of isolation that come with remote working. It builds a sense of connection and means nobody feels invisible. Everyone has the chance to speak about what they need AND to think about each other. People routinely ask, 'what can I do this week to help you?' and act on the answer. It's workable, straightforward and doesn't have to be a big deal. The impact is mega."

If you are not sure how to approach a conversation about how someone is feeling, a sliding scale is a useful aid. At its simplest, the scale goes from 10, 'I'm on top of everything', to 1, 'I'm struggling'.

The questions that go with it are straightforward:

- Where are you on the scale?
- What will it take to move you up?
- What do we need to put in place to stop you moving down?

But remember – there's a secret to making this work. You can't expect people to reveal all if they don't believe that you:

- have their interests at heart and can be trusted not to judge what they tell you;
- want to know the answers, and
- will act on what you agree with them.

When using this tool with teams, the same applies, and there's another dynamic to consider – psychological safety. Team members must be confident that they will not be embarrassed, punished or rejected by the team for speaking the truth as they see it.

The Check-in

The Check-in is helpful in setting the tone for meetings and enabling colleagues to understand each other's perspectives – it can be used one to one, and in groups.

It builds on *Mindful moments* (page 82), and is a powerful tool for groups and teams to use at the start of every meeting.

Ruth Pearce, author of *Be a Project Motivator*, explains why Check-ins are so important. "We are always transitioning from one encounter to another. On projects you go from meeting to meeting, stakeholder to stakeholder, project to project, or task to task. It doesn't matter whether you've been arguing with your significant other, trying to persuade the kids to tidy up, discussing a challenging project issue with the team or delivering news, good or bad, to stakeholders.

To avoid one encounter spilling over into the next, it's helpful to insert a deliberate pause, to get your Thinking brains online and reset your perspective, *before* getting stuck into the work."[2]

Check-ins also help to build psychological safety. We looked at Google's Project Aristotle on page 38. The same project found that there are two hallmarks to a psychologically safe team:[3]

- equality of conversational turn taking, sometimes called 'share of voice'[4]. In psychologically safe teams everyone, including the leader, has roughly the same airtime;
- ostentatious listening – everyone, no matter who they are, listens carefully to what's being said, no matter who is saying it.

To lead a Group Check-in, have a timer to hand, so you can ensure an equal share of voice, and follow the eight steps below.

1. Explain why a Check-in is important, and the need for an equal share of voice and ostentatious listening.
2. Explain that you're going to use the timer to make sure everyone gets equal airtime.
3. Invite people to settle, then lead a *Mindful moments* practice (page 82).
4. Invite people to sit quietly for 30–60 seconds for a Private Check-in.
   Structure the Private Check-in by offering some questions, for example those below:
   - What's your internal weather?
   - How do you feel about being here today?
   - Anything that's on your mind that might get in the way of the work we are about to do together?
   - Any hopes and/or fears?
   Invite people to notice what's coming up as they sit quietly. It might be thoughts, feelings and/or physical sensations.
5. Sharing. Tell the group members that they will each have a pre-set time, say 60, 90 or 120 seconds, to share what came up.
   Their reflections might relate to the task at hand, and they might not. There is no judgement or correct thing to say. I've been at a Check-in where someone spoke about being distracted, because a relative was ill; while someone else felt conflicted, because they were excited about the project but also felt apprehensive and a bit guilty because it would result in job losses.

At another Check-in, where people were invited to speak about their internal weather, one person described a sense of increasing anger, like an approaching storm, while another spoke of a sunny day with the odd cloud scudding across the sky.

6. Use the timer. If somebody does not use all their time, invite them to say more, and encourage the group to sit quietly to allow them the space for other thoughts to arise.
7. When the timer pings, say, 'Thank you', and invite the next person to check in.
8. Check in yourself when everyone else has had a turn. When you do so, remember to ask someone to time you.

Tip: If you have a large group, and you are concerned about the amount of time that a Check-in will take, divide into smaller groups of say three to six people, and do the Check-in within these groups.

Building psychological safety

The Check-in and Taking 10 are useful tools for encouraging people to talk about how they are feeling. Handled well, they can build psychological safety. However, it's often necessary to do more than this by initiating conversations that specifically explore how people are working together – the dynamics.

It's easy to think that this is a straightforward exercise – you simply follow the three steps outlined below. However, these steps will only bring results if people are confident that there will be no repercussions for telling the truth as they see it. This means you need to be careful about:

■ how you gather the data and
■ ensuring that whoever facilitates the follow-up conversation:
   □ can keep their Thinking brain online if emotions run high
   □ knows how to work with groups and teams where there is low psychological safety. (Tell-tale signs of low psychological safety include team members being more concerned about avoiding failure than doing the job well; and team members not daring to speak up about risky or dangerous situations.)

In my experience, in most cases, when first exploring psychological safety, it's not realistic to expect the project leader to lead these discussions without support – they are simply too closely associated with the current way of doing things.

111

If this applies to you, consider engaging a third party, for example an HR partner, project coach, or an external consultant, to gather the results and facilitate the conversation.

Step 1. Gather data.

I do this using a survey of seven statements that come from Amy Edmondson's original research.[5]

a. If you make a mistake on this team, it is often held against you.
b. Members of this team are able to bring up problems and tough issues.
c. People on this team sometimes reject others for being different.
d. It is safe to take a risk on this team.
e. It is difficult to ask other members of this team for help.
f. No one on this team would deliberately act in a way that undermines my efforts.
g. Working with members of this team, my unique skills and talents are valued and utilised.

Ask team members to use a scale to indicate the extent to which they agree with each statement.

Step 2: Collect the data and crunch the numbers.

You might want to use an online tool such as the Psychological Safety Index (PSI), to do this for you.

Step 3: Feed the data back to the team in a facilitated discussion.

☞ The Psychological Safety Index

The PSI has been developed from Amy Edmondson's original seven questions. Team members complete the short questionnaire, and their responses are processed. The results are fed back through a combination of reports and facilitated discussion.

The reports offer a snapshot that puts hard numbers on to the four domains shown in Figure 20.

Inclusion and diversity

When team members feel included, they are more inclined to speak up, contribute and add to the group.

Willingness to help

Team become unsafe when people are not able to help to each other or feel appreciated by team members.

Attitude to risk and failure

Teams that hold mistakes against each other risk a lack of control and forward momentum.

Open conversation

A team that has open and candid conversations is able to tackle hard problems better.

Figure 20 The four PSI domains

Source: Fearless Organization Scan

The numbers make the dynamics tangible. They enable team members to visualise and contrast their experiences of working in the team.

The facilitated discussion enables the team to agree on the areas it wants to address, and how it wants to do so. Joe, a skilled PSI facilitator, describes what happened in one PSI debrief.

Using the PSI: Joe's story

"I'd already done some work with the leader of this tech team, when I was asked to run a session using PSI. I started the session with an explanation of psychological safety and a slide of the four domains. Then I showed them the report of their high-level PSI scores.

The overall score was high, which implied that there was a cluster of people who saw things the same way. But what was interesting was the range – there was quite a big negative deviation and one big outlier.

"The team leader and two real techies were in the cluster with the high PSI. The three of them were responsible for all the big technological innovations, finding new solutions and driving fundamental change.

"It took less than 30 seconds for one of these techies to start talking: 'I'm looking at the consolidated score and at my individual score. I may not be the team leader, but I am the technical leader. I can see that from my perspective there is not an issue of psychological safety in this team. I have absolute confidence in speaking up about anything. But I can also see from the data that there are other members of this team who see things very, very differently. I guess that makes me the *******. From now on, I'm going to shut up and listen, so my colleagues can speak about their experience of psychological safety.'

"To me, as facilitator, that contribution was a gift – one of the most powerful people in the team had invited his colleagues to speak up, and done it in such a way that they knew they would be listened to.

"The person who was the outlier responded immediately. She said, 'You guys are technical experts; I have a very different background. My job is in training and comms. You recruited me because I know about narrative and helping people understand stuff.

"If I'm honest, my experience of being in this team is that you guys, the technical experts, make decisions about what's required very quickly. Then you act on them, and I am the last to know. But here's the thing: I'm the one who's responsible for translating all the stuff that you come up with into words that our customers can understand. My job is to put it into user guides that they can actually use, and this isn't working for me.'

"This exchange led to a lot of dialogue and ultimately a fundamental shift in their strategic approach. The PSI debrief had created an opportunity where she finally felt safe enough, and courageous enough, to bring the voice of the customer into the room."

Now, this is an unusual example, because the shift happened so quickly. More often than not, it takes longer to get to such a pivotal moment, but with quality facilitation you will get there. Once you are there, you have a sound basis for action planning. You also have a PSI baseline, and the option to revisit the survey at a later date to see how PSI scores have changed with actions taken.

If you choose to do a re-measure, it's important to keep in mind the big picture, as things like external pressures, and the addition or loss of team members, may also have an impact – because psychological safety is both dynamic and emergent.

I'm not peddling psychological safety as the answer to everything. Amy Edmondson emphasises that it "takes off the brakes that keep people from achieving what's possible. But it's not the fuel that powers the car ... it spurs learning and avoids preventable failures, but leaders must also set high standards and inspire and enable people to reach them."[6]

The tools we've looked at so far focus primarily on relationships and how to best work with others. It's just as important to focus on 'what you want to achieve together' – the vision and outcomes.

Vision and outcomes

In Part 1, several of the expert practitioners I interviewed spoke about the importance of vision. Many authors have written extensively about it, including Gordon MacKay, who describes vision as one of the triple catalysts of project leadership, alongside insight and foresight as shown in Figure 21.[7]

Some of you may find it hard to reconcile the notion of having a clear vision with the need to embrace uncertainty. If this is you, check out the case studies in Part 4 and take a closer look at Figure 21. Did you spot that one of the catalysts, Insight, focuses on 'how you and the team are working'? How you are working includes how you deal with uncertainty.

Others may have sympathy with Fiona Spencer, whom we met in Part 1. She says: "I'm a bit allergic to the word vision. I've seen a lot of people say they have a vision and wave their arms about. I think it comes down to the question, do they have a clear sense of outcomes they want to deliver? I don't want to be told, 'I

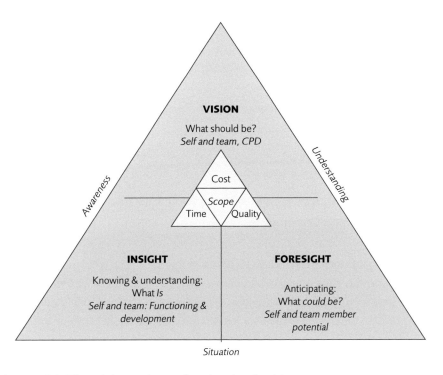

Figure 21 The triple catalysts of project leadership

Source: MacKay[7]

have an ambitious vision'. I want them to give me clarity on what they want to have happened because of this work."

Alexandra Chapman, of Totally Optimized Projects (TOP) in Australia, expands on the difference between vision and outcomes. "Outcomes get you to specifics that go far beyond the vague statements of intent associated with vision. The outcomes process leads to a series of carefully crafted outcomes statements." She goes on to explain: "They describe what the *future* looks like *when it is working just right* (or well, or well enough), and what you *intend* to achieve, and they conform to the principles in Figure 22."

Individually, desired business outcomes are:

1. Specific – they create a clear picture in the mind;

2. What you really want – i.e. they are important to the organisation;

3. Written statements of fact – as if they already exist, in full sentences;

4. Written in the present tense and active voice;

5. Measurable by a true/false question: 'can we/can't we? Do we/don't we?'

6. Without jargon or shorthand;

7. Unambiguous, clear, and specific – they mean the same to everyone (you have to test this!).

Cumulatively, the outcomes:

8. Cover all the dimensions of project output;

9. Describe the end state beyond the project 'go-live';

10. Describe things when they are working 'just right', 'well' or 'well enough'.

Figure 22 10 principles for well-crafted outcome statements
Source: Totally Optimized Projects

According to Alexandra, "Focusing on outcomes gets you away from the situation where business sponsors throw a problem over the wall and hope their project heroes will solve it and where, conversely, project professionals are invited to read the business sponsor's mind and miraculously produce a solution.

"It changes how you measure project success. Success becomes about what you *get out* of the project – your outcomes are the foundation of the project's Value Equation."[i]

Focusing on outcomes changes behaviours. "How many times," she asks, "have you been in a project, or even executive, team meeting where everyone uses the same language but means completely different things? Or where they mean the same thing and say they're on board when they are not? The outcomes process puts a stop to these behaviours. You're either in or you're out; you can't pretend."

To illustrate the need to get to well-crafted outcome statements, Alexandra offers the example of Australia in a Covid lockdown. "Politicians are setting crazy objectives – 'we'll lift restrictions when we get to XX cases a day'.

"If they followed the outcomes process, they would start with something like, 'we cause the minimum harm to people who are not at risk from Covid, and we protect those who are vulnerable to it'. They would go on to refine this statement through a series of tough conversations that culminate in agreement on contentious points such as 'what do we mean by risk?'.

"It takes time to do this because it requires input from many voices, and there is no fudging of difficult conversations. However, it's worth the effort because it gives clarity and confidence in the quality of decision making.

"The process moves you from tacit knowledge, to explicit, codified knowledge." The differences are as follows:

■ Tacit knowledge	■ Each person has something in their head; often it's clear to them, but needs a bit of explaining to others
■ Explicit, codified knowledge	■ A group of people have argued, debated, and got to a reasonable summary.

Alexandra emphasises that the end point, or summary, does not have to be perfect. It needs to be good enough to move forward, and it can take time to reach the shared language of agreement.

To illustrate this, she offers a second example. "When coaching a disability care organisation through the process, we were on version 11 of one outcome statement: *Employees enjoy their work and feel valued each day. They enable*

[i] For more on the Value Equation see, How to generate a Value Equation, available at https://blog.totallyoptimized projects.com/thought-leaders/how-to-generate-a-value-equation (accessed 14 September 2021)

our customers to achieve their goals. On reading this, someone commented: 'You can enjoy working in a bank; what we do means so much more than that.' This set off a lot of debate amongst staff and the leadership team. They reworked the statement several times before reaching agreement at version 14: *Each day is full of joy for our customers and employees. Our employees enable customers to achieve their goals.*

"In this organisation, one word – joy – unlocked a new level of shared understanding and commitment."

Outcome path dependency

Once you've identified your project outcomes, you need to sequence them: 'Because of this ... we can now ...' and 'If we don't have this ... then we can't ...' to identify the outcome path dependency.

Alexandra explains: "Outcome path dependency provides the clarity to make informed decisions about which options to keep open, and which options to close. It cuts out unnecessary work and provides a laser-sharp focus. You simply ask, 'Are we on track with this outcome – Yes, or No?' If it's No, what are you going to do about it? It's not good enough to sit there waiting for something to happen while you carry on spending – maybe you need a major rethink. You should be reviewing progress against outcomes, and the outcomes themselves, frequently; possibly every three months."

She concludes with a warning. "Don't put a small group of, say, 10 people in a room to craft the outcomes statements for your project. They'll probably do a good enough job, but it's about more than the task in a narrow sense. It's also about giving people who are going to be involved in the project, sometimes only in a small way, a voice. They need to feel they were part of the definition process.

"Successful project delivery relies on commitment and intent, and that comes from remembering, often unconsciously, the discussion and debate that went into crafting the outcomes statements."

🔧 The Outcomes Process

We've spoken about the high-level project outcomes. Let's drill down a level and bring the process to life by looking at the extract in Figure 23 of some work I did with a team on recruitment.

Outcome: By 31 March 2021 we've reduced overall staff turnover from ~18% to 10% and the vacancy rate from 25% to 15% at the same time as increasing staff satisfaction.		
Showstopper	**Intermediate outcome**	**Owner**
1. We don't have the figures to benchmark our performance on recruitment against equivalent organisations	1.1 We have benchmarked our recruitment against that of equivalent organisations	AB with JW
	1.2 We have used the benchmark information to set targets for recruitment to each type of post and agreed them at the Management Board	JW
2. Our reputation is not as good as it could be because of historical factors, and we don't know how to make our organisation stand out to potential recruits when there's a national skills shortage	2.1 We have raised our profile with key external groups (e.g. University XX and YY etc)	AB
	2.2 We have engaged with our current staff to understand what they think are the issues in terms of reputation, and junior staff to see what they see as the recruitment & retention pinch points	LQ with staff
	2.3 See 3.1 to 3.4	
	2.3 We have raised our profile internally (e.g. at divisional governance meetings, with operations managers etc)	AB

Figure 23 Outcomes and showstoppers

I used the five-step process below:

1. Agree the headline statement.
2. Identify the showstoppers – the big things you are likely to encounter that will get in your way. (Notice that these are also unambiguous, full sentences, written in the present tense as statements of fact).
3. For each showstopper, identify intermediate outcomes and the owners.
4. Number the intermediate outcomes.
5. Sequence the intermediate outcomes and identify the path dependency.

✎ More uses for outcomes

Clear outcomes are just as important when you're looking at your own development, running a project team meeting or workshop, or even meeting with a stakeholder you've found tricky to deal with in the past. In each of these cases it's important to spend a few minutes ahead of time considering one question: 'How will I know if I've been successful?' In other words, what outcomes do you want?

Let's stay with the tricky stakeholder; it might be tempting to say a good outcome would be something like, 'They are on board for the next phase.'

This might be realistic, or it might be too ambitious – particularly if you've had a history of not working well together. If this is the case, a more realistic approach would be to focus on an outcome that talks directly to that history. For example, 'They believe that I listen to their concerns and that it's possible to have a constructive dialogue.' Achieve this outcome, and you'll be in a better position to get them on board for the next phase.

Consolidating learning and change

We've looked at tools to help us work well with others, and we've looked at tools to keep us focused on the task. It's tempting to say, that should cover it!

But we know from earlier, the human brain is a complex system that is constantly reconfiguring itself in response to changes in the environment. We've also seen:

- how we can encourage the development of new neural pathways through repetition – to build our mindful awareness muscle, for example;
- the power of the stories we tell ourselves, and
- how we can use metaphor and imagery to shift how we think of ourselves, and how we think of those around us.

The same tools and principles apply at a project level.

Look back to Part 1 and you'll see a recurring theme from the expert practitioners I interviewed. The profession struggles with embedding change, sustaining the vision over time, holding to outcomes, and shedding the legacy of command and control.

They use different words, but the theme is clear – *we routinely underestimate what it takes to consolidate learning and change.*

I used to do the same, until two things occurred to me:

- We can use the idea of building and consolidating new neural pathways at both team and organisational level;
- We often undermine ourselves by focusing on the wrong things – our inability to complete a task or achieve a major milestone, for example – rather than

noticing and celebrating the progress (however small or insignificant it seems) that we have made.

One of the tricks of working in a VUCA environment is to keep an eye out for small shifts and changes in behaviours and dynamics, and to create opportunities to talk about them.

I recommend treating each conversation like a still pond, where carefully worded questions are like pebbles. Dropping pebbles into the water creates ripples. Some ripples will merge and build bigger ripples. You can't be 100 per cent sure which are going to coalesce.

However, by asking focused questions and inviting people to talk about the shifts they have made and the changes they have observed, you amplify the ripples. The converse is also true; we pay less attention to things we don't talk about.

One of my favourite tools for encouraging people to notice shifts and amplify changes in the right direction is deceptively simple. It's a single phrase, 'I used to ... and now I'm discovering ...'

✎ I used to ... and now I'm discovering ...

You can use this one phrase in one-to-ones, stand-ups, regular team meetings, workshops and even for self development. Notice how the sentence construction forces you to broaden your perspective; how far, depends on the timescale you choose. I might use it when asking a coachee to look back two or 12 weeks, or even to a time when they couldn't even contemplate something, so they can see their progress.

It's just as helpful with a team when the goalposts have moved, and there's a sense of being stuck. In this case it's helpful to:

1. Give team members five minutes alone to look back over the last six months, for example, and to identify all the 'I used to ... and now I'm discovering ... instances.
2. Invite them to share their answers in groups of three or four for 20 minutes and to come up with group learnings.
3. Share small group learnings with the wider team.
4. And if you want to, you can amplify the ripples further by asking the team to consider:
   □ 'Given what we've discovered, where do we feel most exposed now?
   □ 'What else should we be looking for?'

Can you see how clarity of intention and the careful choice of words and language make all the difference when you want to consolidate change and learning? It's a theme that we pick up in the Akamai case study in Part 4.

Takeaways

- Once you have learned to bring your own Thinking brain online, and identify how you are contributing to the situation, you will be well placed to look outside yourself and:
  - □ Recognise when others' Thinking brains are offline.
  - □ Make informed choices about the behaviours and interventions required to bring them back online.
  - □ See systemic patterns such as: How psychologically safe is it? What's the dominant orientation – certainty or uncertainty? How is stress playing out across the system?
  - □ Take a view on if, and how, to intervene.
- The ideas and tools introduced in earlier chapters can be adapted and used to address systemic patterns that relate to how people work together.
- It's not enough to focus all your effort on the 'how' of working together. You also need to attend to what you want to achieve together – the vision and, in particular, outcomes.

Vision and outcomes

- Outcomes get you to specifics that go far beyond the vague statements of intent associated with vision.
- An outcomes statement describes what the future looks like when it's working *just right* (well or well enough) and what you *intend* to achieve.
- Outcomes statements conform to the 10 principles set out in Figure 22.
- The outcomes process moves you from tacit knowledge to explicit, codified knowledge. Rather than each person having 'something in their head which they can't quite explain', a group of people have argued, debated and got to a reasonable summary.
- Successful project delivery relies on the commitment and intent that comes from remembering, often unconsciously, the discussion and debate that went into crafting the outcomes statements.

Consolidating learning and change

- We routinely underestimate what it takes to consolidate learning and change.
- We can overcome this by remembering that, like the brain-body combo, organisations are complex systems.
- The techniques we've explored for building and consolidating new neural pathways at an individual level, apply at a team and organisational level too.
- Rather than undermining ourselves by over-focusing on the wrong things (our inability to complete a task or achieve a major milestone, for example), we need to set out with the intention of noticing and celebrating small shifts and progress (however insignificant).
- We can influence how the system evolves, and project success, by making wise choices about which messages and stories to amplify, and which to dampen.

References

1 Osterweil, C. *How do you Manage an Invisible Workforce* IT NOW, March 2021, p50–51
2 4 Steps to Labeling Emotions for Project Managers, available at https://projectmotivator.com/labeling-emotions-lessons-learned-from-in-it-together-group-coaching/(accessed 2 September 2021)
3 How Google builds the perfect team, available at https://www.youtube.com/watch?v=v2PaZ8Nl2T4&list=PLhVoCCkYxQDcdcU7j7H_w0-0BdOqIIYxa&t=6s, (accessed 2 Sept 2021)
4 Marquet, D. (2020), *Leadership is Language: The hidden power of what you say and what you don't,* UK, Penguin Business, p33
5 Edmondson, A. (2019), *The Fearless Organization: creating psychological safety in the workplace for learning innovation and growth,* New Jersey, Wiley p20
6 Edmondson, A. (2019), *The Fearless Organization: creating psychological safety in the workplace for learning innovation and growth,* New Jersey, Wiley p21
7 MacKay, G. (2021), *Evolving Project Leadership,* Association for Project Management, p83

Part 4. Integrating neuroscience into your projects

9

Case studies

The preceding chapters have offered you new ideas, tools and mini-case studies. In writing them, I have been encouraging you to look through a pair of binoculars, with the eye-piece focused primarily on what you, as an individual, can do to influence your teams, stakeholders and project delivery.

As we move into Part 4, I want to flip the binoculars and invite you to look at the world through the opposite lens: what happens at the project and organisational level, when the ideas we explored earlier inform everything you do?

I answer this question with four case studies, covering projects that differ enormously in terms of sector, geography, scale, duration and challenge. Separately and together, they give you a window onto how successful project leaders have applied neuroscience, and used many of the frameworks and tools I introduced earlier, to change their whole organisation's approach to delivery.

If you are not used to flipping the binoculars and moving from the systemic to the personal, you might want to check out the suggestions in Appendix B.

Either way, you can read the case studies in order, or start with the one that seems most pertinent for the challenges you face.

- Project initiation and delivery: Belfast Transport Hub, Translink
- Cultural change: introducing a Growth Mindset at Akamai Technologies, Inc.
- Smoothing the way in a merger of government departments
- Walking in Fog: leading the UK Vaccine Taskforce.

Project initiation and delivery: Belfast Transport Hub, Translink

The Belfast Transport Hub (BTH) is one of the largest single investments in Northern Ireland's history. Taking shape at Weavers Cross, it's a city-centre site that includes the existing Europa Bus Centre and Great Victoria Street train station. BTH is the catalyst for a wider regeneration programme that aims to attract 8,000 new jobs and £1bn investment into Belfast by 2035.

Duncan McAllister, programme head, talks about the challenges of delivering a construction and redevelopment programme in a live, operational environment where 20 million bus and rail passengers a year don't want their journeys interrupted. All in the context of a post-conflict society where political instability continues.

He picks up the story in November 2019, when contracts had been signed and the initial phases of delivery had just commenced. Contractors were onsite for the £20m enabling works, and procurement for the main construction contract had begun. In parallel, the team had started the initiation phase for the redevelopment programme, and were working on its vision.

Business change

Alongside construction, we knew there would be a big element of business change in the operations side of the business[i] and corporate functions[ii]. The programme would impact their work in ways they hadn't seen before.

For example, when we started out, we took the view that collaboration with potential construction partners was crucial to success. We wanted to encourage discussion and dialogue by bringing suppliers to site, to show them the location of work, brief them about expectations, and explore the project's complexities.

When we first spoke about introducing this level of collaboration, we'd be told, 'that's not possible'. People weren't resistant to the idea – they were anxious about things being taken out of context and the potential risk of a challenge to the competition. They couldn't quite see how it could be done while remaining compliant with the procurement and contractual assurance procedures for a scheme of this size. We've now worked with internal teams to demonstrate that it is possible.

As a result, we've seen many benefits. It's led to systems and approaches that incorporate best practice while maintaining the commercial tension to ensure competitive, quality bids. It's supported early relationship building with suppliers and a clearer understanding of our needs and expectations.

We can be open and frank, with our main works contractor and their supply chain, saying: 'We can only do so much as the client. We need your input to find solutions and take us to the next stage of delivery.' This has brought groundbreaking innovations. They've risen to the challenge and linked directly

[i] Includes Rail, Bus, Engineering, and other departments
[ii] Contracts, procurement etc

with our operational and corporate teams – who have responded by adapting and changing culture to arrive at a solution that works.

The introduction of new technology into BTH illustrates a very different challenge. For this to succeed, we invited people with operational expertise to act as business change ambassadors and champions. Their role is to help the project team understand the constraints of keeping the buses and trains running around the clock; and to ensure the operations team understand, a) what a construction project of this scale looks like, and b) how it can have a long-term positive impact on bus and train services.

This focus on the long-term gain is vital in counterbalancing the short-term pain and disruption that comes with each set of operational changes required as we move through the programme.

The risk of a toxic culture: mitigation management

The project team knew we were being ambitious, and that we had a relentless and time-sensitive programme. It was challenging enough to have multidisciplinary teams pushing for planning while we were advancing procurement matters and in parallel designing new solutions for delivery of the final station and operational areas.

But that wasn't all we had to contend with. Additional pressure came from knowing we were under the spotlight – this was the largest infrastructure project the business had delivered to date. What's more, it was the first time Translink had done anything on this scale of complexity and disruption to a live operation, or over such a long period of time.

We could see that everyone was going to be under a lot of personal and professional pressure. We couldn't deliver without the people, and we recognised the risk of team burnout. This could lead to a toxic culture, and getting trapped in the dynamics of the Project Stress Cycle. We concluded that protecting mental health and wellbeing was vital.

Mental health and wellbeing

Translink already had a mental health and wellbeing initiative in place, and had set up processes to encourage employees to adopt a mindfulness approach. This platform was the natural starting point for addressing our concerns.

We linked to it by establishing project mental health and wellbeing champions, and being explicit with team leaders and members about uncertainty. The BTH team would experience a sustained period of flux; we would all need to embrace the change when it arrived, and adapt to the new normal as quickly as possible.

We focused time and effort on three strands of work to ensure they understood the implications:

- Mindfulness and the Growth Mindset
- Constructive Collaboration
- Community Connections

Fortunately, we'd already kicked off the first two strands when Covid struck. They helped us enormously in navigating the additional uncertainty that came with soaring infection rates, lockdowns and working from home.

Mindfulness and the Growth Mindset

We explained to the team that the pressure would come in waves, and we discussed how mindfulness and the Growth Mindset could support them. We wanted them to personally understand how these approaches could help them think more clearly when under pressure. Part of this was training, and part of it was an exploration: how would they cope individually, and how would they cope as a team?

Mindfulness training

We took advantage of the existing Translink campaign and said to the team: 'As part of your CPD this year, you're expected to attend eight, one-hour mindfulness sessions over the next six months. It will help you deliver professionally over the next five years, and it will help you at a personal level.'

Many of the team have done more than eight sessions. They report it has helped them in thinking differently; in their interactions with colleagues, partners, and children; and in dealing with the extra pressure of balancing work and home life during lockdowns.

We also recognised that getting such a diverse and disparate team to work really well together would bring challenges. We addressed this by engaging an external organisation to support us in fostering psychological safety, through the provision of a structured process and facilitated meetings.

Constructive Collaboration

The organisation, Constructive Collaboration, has worked on lots of large and complex public and private sector infrastructure projects. Their framework is set up to encourage openness and honesty about what's not working, and why – at a team and an individual level.

The process

The BTH team sets aside a full day every two months for a team review. The morning focuses on successes to share, what's working well and the problems we are facing. The afternoon is dedicated to continuous improvement, through focused group work on specific knotty project issues – around better communication to the wider team, or commercial management, for example.
We don't try to do this in 45 minutes, crammed in before the next meeting. We see the value of slowing everything down and working issues through with others, in a way that empowers everyone to become part of the solution.

As this way of working has become more embedded, we've seen early sceptics become some of its biggest fans. We are less reliant on independent facilitation. Teams are working on their own, in workstream areas, to drive even more collaboration.

The third strand of work, Community Connections, builds on the first two strands and integrates them. With a focus on realising social and economic value, it has become one of the main pillars of the benefits realisation scheme in our business case.

Community Connections

This strand enables team members to understand that their work has an impact beyond operations – this project has the power to change lives by connecting people, place and opportunity. It recognises that we are in a post-conflict society where political instability continues. We need to deal with the legacy of conflict by looking to the current and future needs of Northern Ireland.

Community Connections enables us to engage closely with key stakeholders in the city, mainly our closest residential neighbours. It acknowledges that a programme of this scale inevitably disrupts their lives and livelihoods. Despite this, they have the potential to be engaged supporters; the programme will run for 20 years and, in this time, it will create many jobs. We like to say, 'Your children are potential employees of the businesses we will create through the Belfast Transport Hub and the wider Weavers Cross Regeneration project.'

Focused on community events and social and economic value, ambassadors from our team:

- Speak to the community about their jobs and their role in delivering the programme. The aim is to build trust and the understanding to provide the foundation for long term, sustainable relationships by demonstrating that we care about enhancing lives and livelihoods.
- Create opportunities to work with the community through the donation of time, labour, resources and skills. One example of this is a Community Day: team members went into a local primary school to paint the classrooms and corridors, easing the burden on the school's budget. This led to a new narrative about our work in the wider community: 'These people have taken time off work to do things that make a huge difference to our young people and their education – things that we can't get funding for.'

Community engagement has given team members a real sense of purpose and new perspectives. They can now picture what it's like to be one of the refugee children in a local school who's lost their family in a war zone and been rehoused with strangers; or a single parent who lives less than a mile from our site offices and is trying to bring up children on a low income while struggling with social issues or mental health.

We see a new level of motivation driven by a crystal-clear vision – 'I'm doing this job for that 11, 12 or 13 year old, who will be 16, 17 or 18 when we've finished the project. My work is connecting them to the wider community and potential employment and education. I can make a difference to society by bringing this project into operation.'

Embedding change

It's not enough to focus on one of these strands, or to think 'I've done that strand – job done.'

Taken together, the three strands have made the team resilient. When people encounter difficulties, they stand up and are open and honest about vulnerability, and the problems they face.

We've learned that we must continually reinforce the strands and remind ourselves and others: 'This is where we were; this is what we did about it; we can go there again, and adopt a continuous improvement practice.'

Sometimes that's hard to do – you get swept up by the tidal wave, and you've got to keep on extracting yourself. You have to stop, take your time, and regroup. It's about creating the conditions to think logically – without the emotional side of your brain taking over and pushing you into 'make a decision' mode.

Where are we now?

We met the original objectives for this phase of the project and submitted a full business case in August 2021. Since then, we've continued with the collaborative approach and rigorous attention to applying lessons learned. We've updated the full business case to account for the continued impact of Covid and Brexit on Northern Ireland, and to include an assessment of the global market factors that are in a high state of change. These documents were well received, and our business case has been signed off by our government sponsors.

We have achieved this through a constant focus on embedding mental health and wellbeing, mindfulness, collaboration and connection, and by facing issues in 'can-do, will-do' solution mode. This focus has supported us through everything we've delivered to date.

Cultural change: introducing Growth Mindset at Akamai Technologies Inc.

In December 2018, executives at Akamai Technologies Inc. decided it was time to act. Their employee pulse survey highlighted an area of concern. Bill Bangs, organisational change management director at the tech company explains.

"Staff told us we needed to improve at anticipating change, and we needed to adapt even faster. Employees wanted the organisation to be more agile.

"The question was how? We're a project-based organisation, we're big in cyber security and cloud solutions and we have a strong engineering culture. We couldn't get away with something fluffy; our approach needed to be grounded in robust scientific evidence.

Fortunately, several leaders in our Global Talent Development organisation had close ties to the NeuroLeadership Institute (NLI), an organisation that uses science to help organisations be more adaptive, resilient and inclusive. In 2019, with their help, we kicked off a two-year change programme, and we've benefited in many ways. It had just got underway when the pandemic struck. There's no doubt that it has helped with resilience and enabled us to pivot rapidly to becoming almost exclusively virtual/remote.

At the programme level, we collect data using the Behavioural Change Percentage (BCP)[1] and our pulse survey, to get a sense of the impact of this work. It wasn't long before we started to see positive results.

Behavioural Change Percentage

BCP measures how frequently employees and managers perform a new and desired behaviour.

For example, Akamai asks managers: 'how often have you displayed a Growth Mindset this week?' and staff: 'how often has your manager displayed a Growth Mindset this week?'

Goal: Module 1 training will lead participants to actively shift from a Fixed to a Growth Mindset at least one to three times per week. Target benchmark: 60 per cent or better.

Result from surveys: 80 per cent of participants shifted from a Fixed to a Growth Mindset at least once a week.

Based on pulse survey results, employees have seen improvements in our ability to anticipate and adapt. We've also seen improvements against our BCP baseline. But that's not all. We regularly use BCP to benchmark ourselves against industry standards for the programme modules, and we're delighted to see we've been consistently above the industry benchmarks.

What's in the programme?

The core is an modular course that we've rolled out to executives, managers and individual contributors. It covers four themes.

- GROW – the neuroscience of a Growth Mindset
  - What makes us behave the way we do? Do you view changes as a threat or opportunity? Focus on continual learning, improve NOT prove.

- INCLUDE – the neuroscience of smarter teams
  - ☐ How can we become more inclusive? The need to belong, Ingroups and Outgroups. Understanding the impact of social domains, using SCARF.
- DECIDE – the neuroscience of breaking bias
  - ☐ How can we mitigate unconscious biases – in business decisions (what are we going to invest in?), and people decisions (how we approach hiring, promotions and performance reviews)?
- VOICE – the neuroscience of speaking up
  - ☐ How can we develop psychological safety so people will say what's on their mind? (They might not get their way every time, but let's ensure people have a voice and are actually heard).

Its focus is on building habits through bite-sized inputs. Each module takes less than half a day and introduces three habits, but the real value comes from embedding these habits through paying attention to them, repetition and reinforcement. We layer the habits and go back to them again and again, in modules, between modules and in communications across the business.

In the modules

To give a micro-level example, one of the core habits in our VOICE module is 'Noticing the Moment'. So, when facilitating this module, we might say, 'This week, why not focus on Noticing the Moment – try writing down when you feel uncomfortable, about something that you heard (an idea or a decision) or something that you see, a behaviour that's very hard to talk to someone about ... and perhaps pair up with an accountability partner, a colleague from the programme who will support you and challenge you to follow through on your intentions.'

We also focus on reinforcement and ask people for examples of what they've been up to. When they answer, we often need to point out how their behaviour is shifting, because they often are not aware of it. It's 'Guess what, when you pivoted there, you were actually displaying a Growth Mindset. It doesn't make what you did before wrong; you don't have to have a Growth Mindset 100 per cent of the time – but you did just then.'

It's the interaction, attention to detail and follow-through that makes the learning sticky.

Between the modules

They follow up with their accountability partners, but it doesn't stop there. We're also supporting the culture change through the work of Change Champions, known as our Grow Ambassadors – volunteers within the business whose role is to model the behaviours locally and support others in making the changes. As they do this, change starts to happen organically. People locally may not even be aware of the Change Champion's intention to model behaviours, but they copy the behaviours anyway.

Our executives also play an important role by modelling the behaviours and using the new language – you really see this in the blogs they put out when undertaking new initiatives. We also constantly hear mention of 'Growth Mindset' from our executives when they're addressing our employees, from town halls, all hands and staff meetings. It's become a part of our culture.

We've been lucky – our timing couldn't have been better; we'd just completed GROW and were in the middle of INCLUDE when the pandemic struck. This meant that our executives and managers could frame the challenges of the pandemic and the move to 100 per cent virtual in terms of a Growth Mindset. Like everyone else we encountered some setbacks when making the change. But we overcame those quickly, because people could look at things differently, and say, 'We don't have to be perfect – let's go ahead and aim to continually learn and improve.' That mindset meant we learned together and could talk about things we tried that worked, as well as the difficulties we faced.

Communications across the business

Recently, as with most companies, we've faced a challenge of having some employees struggling to maintain balance due to the blurred lines between work and home life. This programme is helping us pause and consider mental health. People now know to ask, 'How are you feeling?' and they are using the learning from the SCARF model (covered extensively in the INCLUDE and VOICE modules), '... you're feeling that your choices are taken away, that's an autonomy threat. How can we change it to a reward? Where else might we look to identify where you do have choices?'

We see the impact in our business planning. When talking about next year's budgets, there are conversations about which projects to take on and which to stop, and included in these conversations, we now see discussions about how to avoid unconscious bias.

We see it when people are running late on delivery. In the past, employees might have been quite anxious and saying, 'We've got to fix this.' Now we're seeing evidence of a better sense of perspective and we're hearing managers tell their teams, 'Let's look at how far we've come over the last six months', which can help put people in a reward state where they can better collaborate and be creative. Then it's: 'OK, let's be realistic; we're about a week behind. Let's think of some ideas about how to recover it. Maybe we can ...'

It's also changed how employees perceive issues logs. People are more open to opportunities and don't see every issue as a threat anymore. Sometimes 'issues' are actually opportunities to innovate. People talk about experimenting, taking risks and being ready for things not to work first time.

When it comes to meetings, people have more intent and spend time thinking about how to structure them better. In status meetings, we're beginning to see teams spending less time reporting where they're at (with scope, schedule and budget), and more time collaborating on questions and discussions of what to do, with space for introverts to think things through and contribute.

Where next?

The programme's ambition is for the Grow Ambassadors to take even more ownership for helping employees to adopt new inclusive behaviours, especially as the formal, two-year roll-out of the modules comes to an end.

Lynn Hare, a director within Akamai's Global Talent Development group, says: "In line with our Growth Mindset, our GROW programme does not have an end destination – our focus is on progression and successes. We are constantly learning, and new science is continually being realised, and as we connect those new ideas to Akamai's needs, we will introduce additional modules to Akamai employees to continue this journey. We are currently working on a programme to sustain and further embed the habits of the first four modules, but we are also exploring new modules for 2022. Our Grow Ambassadors will continue to play an important part in our journey, and we will be further leveraging their passion and drive, to more independently role model the organisational and personal benefits of embracing the habits of GROW."

Bangs adds: "It's about sustaining the gains. I'd like to see them develop more materials based on their experiences of working in this way, and use those materials to amplify the messages. I want it to become like software – when companies started with open-source and put it out to the world, it led to amazing innovation."

Smoothing the way in a merger of government departments

Mergers and takeovers are never easy, whether they are in the corporate or public sector. Here we tell the story of introducing a new programme operating framework to over 12,000 staff, following the merger of two government departments (referred to in this anonymised case study as P and X).

Neeta, the programme lead, picks up the story. When they announced the merger, I was unusual because, as a fairly new arrival, I didn't have a particularly strong attachment to my existing organisation, P. Almost everybody else was against the idea of a merger. People on both sides thought the other side would be taking over, and there were lots of very complex human emotions at play.

'Deliver the framework – deal with the people stuff'

My job was to use my project and programme management expertise to deliver the programme operating framework for the merged organisation, Phoenix. At this point, it didn't have much definition – it was simply 'the thing that Phoenix would use to hold itself to account'. Apart from this, I had seven months until the go-live date, and I knew that successful delivery depended on 'dealing with the people stuff'.

The two organisations had completely different traditions in programme delivery. Programme delivery was strongly embedded in P's culture; it was 'what P did'. With a budget of over £9bn, P's staff saw themselves as programme delivery experts.

In contrast, X also had a budget for programmes, but it was a fraction of P's. Most of the staff in X would say their work had nothing to do with programmes. People in X wanted the metrics and structure that come with projects and programmes, but they had never generated the momentum to make it happen. They viewed programming as 'something other people do'.

My job was to reconcile these two traditions and to come up with a framework that would work for people from both sides.

Providing a haven

I knew they had to buy into the framework, understand it, and be part of making it. But how in the world were we going to develop it, test it and convince them that it was the right thing to do when everything, including governance, was constantly shifting and evolving?

I've done lots of transformation programmes before, but this was much more visceral. I felt vulnerable and exposed. If it went wrong, it would be my problem.

With so much animosity, it was obvious that success hinged on making the transformation about the people. We needed to be professional, knowledgeable and competent, but that wouldn't be enough. We needed to put people at the centre of the framework's design.

Crucially, we made a commitment at the outset that we'd create the framework by listening. And we recognised that, in this climate, it was vital to demonstrate that we could be trusted to provide a haven of psychological safety in very rough seas.

How we got through

That seven months was the biggest test of resilience I've ever experienced, and I've done a lot of challenging things. Initially I struggled because we were spending so much time just talking. I had to repeatedly remind myself that we needed to build relationships and rapport, and that meant resisting my desire for action.

The notion of Walking in Fog helped enormously. It gave me permission to feel uncertain and not to know what was going to happen next.

Walking in Fog

I would often refer to Walking in Fog to keep the team and stakeholders focused. 'This is a foggy phase, there are lots of unknowns, but we'll work our way through. We can make progress and move forward; we don't need to fix everything for the next phase to be different.' This was my constant refrain, and they found it very reassuring.

Equally, when we were riding high and everything was going smoothly, I could set expectations that things would get tricky again. This realism gave us the confidence to continue, despite the difficulties.

And there were difficulties and new stresses – almost every day. In addition to the ambitious objective and timeline, we had Covid, which brought its own uncertainties. Not least, a reliance on video interaction, which meant people were often less nuanced than they would be face-to-face.

Dealing with stress

Knowing I needed to keep my Thinking brain online really helped. I'd be sitting at my desk, thinking, 'Don't lose it. Breathe in. Calm. Keep your Feeling brain in check'. This was vital for several reasons.

In high-stress situations, my reflex used to be to shut other people out and focus on *my* plan. Using the *Mindful moments* technique stopped me getting tunnel vision, locking on to my solution, and missing important contributions from others.

In addition, we were making it up as we went along and had to think everything through. Being emotional gets in the way of considering tricky questions like, 'How can we keep interpersonal friction at a minimum while providing space for the productive friction that will enable both sides to compromise?'

One of the approaches that helped broker difficult conversations was using visuals, as these helped people talk about where they were coming from and what they were experiencing.

Imagery to broker difficult conversations

For example, in one set of virtual meetings we wanted to surface what people felt about the two organisations coming together. To explore this, we invited attendees to draw and share a picture. We got a huge range of images, from a pancake to little children curled up in balls. It was so interesting to hear people talking about anger and disappointment while drawing pictures that were about vulnerability.

We could do this because we'd worked hard to build a safe and caring environment, where people could talk about the difficult stuff without being aggressive or abusive. Having this type of conversation allowed us to build a sense of care and support that went beyond me and the management team. It created opportunities for individuals to connect, share and support each other independently.

Focusing on the vision and outcomes

The word 'framework' is abstract, so when times were tough, it was vital to have a clear vision and sense of outcomes to come back to. I would tell people to imagine a worker who spoke English as their fourth or fifth language, using the framework. This 'thing' would cover everything from climate change to financial probity, and it would be far more than a set of rules and instructions. Colleagues across the globe would see it as a one-stop shop to support them in finding answers to their 'How shall we approach this?' questions.

Take one example, safeguarding. Every programme run by Phoenix needs to protect the people involved, whether they are delivering it or benefiting from it. The framework is designed to help anyone on the team to work out what needs to happen to safeguard against sexual exploitation and harassment on one hand, and to provide a route for escalating risks, issues and whistleblowing on the other.

Success would be measured by engagement – do people want to use the framework?

Do people want to use the framework?

At the time of writing, it looks promising. The framework was launched after a consultation phase that touched around 5,000 people. We started out by seeking feedback from several hundred, before we opened the doors more widely and spoke to everyone who wanted to engage. Around 2,000 people attended sessions in the run-up to the launch and, even then, we were taking on information and honing the framework.

We set out with a commitment to listen, and we've lived up to it. Many people have reported that their voice has been heard. It's been wonderful to receive this feedback, because there was so much animosity when I started this project that part of me didn't believe we could pull it off.

Walking in Fog: leading the UK Vaccine Taskforce

In spring 2020, when the Vaccine Taskforce (VTF) was set up, Covid infection rates were growing exponentially in the UK. No one really understood the virus and uncertainty was rife. Unusually, uncertainty was part of the public discourse.

Nick Elliott, senior responsible officer (SRO) and sponsor for the VTF, describes what happened.[2]

Three big, audacious goals

The programme was set up with three goals. The first was to secure access to a promising Covid-19 vaccine, or vaccines, for the UK population as quickly as possible. This meant selecting the right vaccines to pursue, ensuring the manufacturing capability was in place to deliver them and doing the right commercial deals. Most important was to do all of this at a rapid pace.

The second goal was to make provision for the international distribution of vaccines, as we recognised that getting a solution for the UK was only part of the plan. The third was a legacy goal to support the UK industrial strategy by establishing a long-term vaccine strategy to prepare the UK for future pandemics, especially in terms of UK manufacturing.

The only way to achieve this was to set out from the start a clear vision of what success looked like and to be absolutely focused on delivering that outcome.

This meant getting a team together quickly. It was not a traditional team, but a 'rainbow' team of scientific and industry experts, civil servants, military planners and a few consultants. Within a few months there were around 200 people working together. Based in the Department of Business, Energy and Industrial Strategy (BEIS), we had to go through all the government processes, procedures and approvals to get anything done.

Following process was important to ensure accountability of how we were spending taxpayers' money. However, speed of action was mission-critical – we needed to navigate that process in a way that allowed us to operate at the pace we needed. We needed to focus on outcomes rather than procedures and to do this at speed.

The answer was to design bespoke governance and to build trust and confidence with all the key decision makers across all of government, but especially in the Treasury, Cabinet Office and Number 10, and it was about making sure we had an absolutely robust and focused plan against which success could be measured.

Agility through necessity

We found lots of ways to be agile. For example, we had to get approval from four different departments to spend any money; even after we had our portfolio budget approved by the Treasury, we needed sign-off from four ministers. Normally, going through those four different departments and all their teams and briefers would take considerable time and effort. So, we got them to agree to come together in a single ministerial panel: the four of them together with one set of papers – and we could call them together at 24 hours' notice. They were fantastically flexible.

This meant that in one example we closed the negotiation late on a Monday night, we put it through the BEIS internal approvals processes by the Thursday, we called the panel together on the Friday evening and by Saturday we had signed the contract. Four-and-a-half days from completion of a contract negotiation to signing is unheard-of in government.

Placing bets

When we started, there were more than 200 potential vaccines undergoing some form of development – so how did we decide where to place our bets? Rigorous expert assessment was hugely important, and so was using the right selection criteria. We wanted a range of different vaccine types from the traditional, inactivated whole virus vaccine, to the new, and novel, mRNA types. But the most important criterion was time: was the vaccine already in the clinic, could it get to human trials quickly, and could it be manufactured at pace to ensure it would be available if and when it was proved safe and effective and approved for use?

Not only did we need to decide which vaccines to back, but also where to invest at risk on trials capacity and manufacture. There was a worldwide shortage of manufacturing capacity. So putting this into place for the UK, without knowing at that stage exactly which vaccine it was going to be used for, was another critical successful factor.

Once we had selected our portfolio, we needed to start negotiations. This is not commodity procurement of drugs; we needed to build partnerships and alliances with the companies we wanted to work with, and each and every one of those was very different. For example, the deal with Oxford University and AstraZeneca was for a vaccine developed in the UK with government investment; Oxford had then brought in AstraZeneca with government support. We put in place government-funded manufacturing capacity and agreed a not-for-profit/not-for-loss deal that also promoted international manufacture and distribution. This was a very different negotiation to the Pfizer-BioNTech vaccine, which had been produced without any initial investment from the UK. Given the unique distribution challenges of the -70 degrees centigrade cold chain of this vaccine, the joint development of a supply and distribution solution between the UK and Pfizer became a key part of the deal.

Ending on a high

At the end of November 2020, the Pfizer-BioNTech Phase 3 trial results arrived. They proved the vaccine to be safe and effective. It was an absolutely amazing moment. We'd never known, until that point, whether or not we could even have a vaccine, and to have the first one proven to be so successful was quite amazing.

By 2 December 2020 the UK had approved that vaccine – the first country in the world to do so – and by 8 December, just one week later, Margaret Keenan was the first person to receive it. Within a three-week period, we'd gone from trial results, through regulatory approval, to distribution and deployment.

References

1 Neuroleadership Institute (2021), *Growth Mindset Supports Organizations Through Disruption*, available at https://hub.neuroleadership.com/growth-mindset-impact-report (accessed 12 September 2021).
2 Elliott, N. Running the UK's vaccination taskforce, *Project*, Summer 2021 p39–41

10

Overturning command and control

This book started with some big statements:

- We need to reduce the number of projects that fail – in every sector.
- We've been asking people to deliver huge projects, with big people impacts, for years, and we haven't given them a model that clearly explains 'why people behave as they do' – it's crazy!

I went on to observe that this isn't surprising, because until recently a robust model to explain why people behave as they do did not exist. However, this is no longer the case. Advances in neuroscience have filled that gap.

I hope you've discovered from reading the preceding chapters, and experimenting with the tools in them, that starting from the inside with an understanding of how the human brain works really does equip you to successfully navigate the unpredictable world of project delivery.

I hope you can also see that, if we want our projects to succeed, we cannot continue to focus most of our effort (and training), on the processes for designing, planning and coordinating the delivery of projects, while assuming others – those pesky stakeholders, team members and end users – will fall in with our plans, because we've told them to do so with volume and vigour.

Now we have a robust model to explain why people behave as they do, it's immediately obvious that this assumption is fundamentally flawed. In fact, the opposite is true!

All processes for designing, planning and coordinating the delivery of projects must *start* with the assumption that we need to do the work that will make it possible for others to willingly join us, and collaborate, in our project endeavours.

If they don't want to, it will be nothing to do with resistance to change. It will be because we've not paid enough attention to their very human needs, and we've inadvertently set off an avoidance response.

Yes, it's all about moving away from a 'command and control' to an 'empower and engage' model of leadership. And it's more than that.

Neuroscience for project success

The authors of *Project Resilience* explain: "We are constantly challenged by expectations of certainty and thus control. We vote for people who sell us an illusory world of stability, predictability and wellbeing. In turn, we expect others to plan and control the future, and project owners and sponsors also expect that of us. To put your hand up and argue that the world out there is largely unknowable is a daunting task. Anyone who's trying to 'sell' a project knows that it's more advantageous to pitch it as (reasonably) certain. Presenting your plan as largely unpredictable, but nonetheless resilient, is a tougher prospect. Even if both the audience and the presenter, deep down, realise that there are aspects that remain unknowable, it is more comforting to go with a confident, traditional, planned approach. Of course, as long as this remains the case, the life of the project manager is likely to be challenging."[1]

There you have it. There's an inherent conflict between what we know deep down on the inside, and the pull to conform to expectations and stay with the comfortable, if illusory, world of certainty and control promised by traditional approaches to project management and leadership.

I concluded Chapter 2 on page 21 with the reflection that, as a profession, we know that command and control is an out-dated approach, and we are *grappling with its pull and its legacy in lots of ways*.

In writing this book I knew I'd be going out on a limb and introducing ideas that would be exciting to some readers and appear far-fetched for others. Wherever you are on this spectrum, Appendix A shows that what I've written is consistent with the latest thinking from the professional bodies.

In concluding this book, I want to illustrate how material from earlier chapters talks to my point; we need to go beyond thinking about command and control solely in terms of a leadership model. We also need to deal with its pull and its legacy.

As I say this, the proverb, 'the fish are the last to discover water', springs to mind. Many of us who work on projects have grown up in the world of command and control, and we take its constraints for granted.

The fish are the last to discover water

Everything we learned in Chapters 3 and 4 reinforces this point of view. We are wired for survival and we're social creatures. Our need to belong is so strong that in environments of questionable psychological safety our reflex is to keep quiet, even if this means denying our truth and going along with irrational decisions and dysfunctional behaviours that work against the best interests of project delivery.

What's more, as the disconnect between meeting expectations of control and being true to ourselves increases, it becomes harder to keep our Thinking brains online. This impacts trust, communication and the quality of risk assessment and decision making. It also leads to an increase in complexity and more stress, eventually creating systemic issues like the Project Stress Cycle and a drift towards a toxic culture.

As a profession we've recognised that moving from command and control to empower and engage means developing people's emotional intelligence and their skills to create psychologically safe environments.

We saw in Chapter 5 that advances in neuroscience have added another dimension to this quest. Emotional intelligence starts inside, with learning to regulate ourselves so we can regulate others.

Daniel Goleman realised the importance of self-awareness and self-management in the 1990s, when he put these two domains at the heart of his influential model of emotional intelligence. At that time, understanding of how the brain works and why people behave as they do was far less developed.

As a result, although we've seen substantial investment in building the emotional intelligence of the project management community to facilitate movement towards an engage and empower model of leadership, we have not realised the potential of this approach.

How could we? Neuroscience research was still in its infancy, and most people thought that self-awareness, the foundation stone of emotional intelligence, was about getting an outside view in the form of feedback from others.

Chapters 5 and 7 showed that feedback from others is only part of the self-awareness story. It's a useful part, but not the main part. That, I argue, is about learning to lead from the inside out, by developing a strong mindful awareness muscle, and the ability to access somatic intelligence.

When we can press the pause button, and use this intelligence to make sense of, and talk about, our physical and emotional responses, we'll be better able to keep our Thinking brains online. We'll stop inadvertently adding layers of stress and complexity to project delivery, and we'll be able to see what's really going on with clarity. This in turn will allow us to make informed choices about interacting with the outside world – where to focus and how to respond to the challenges we face.

One of the key challenges we face is overturning the legacy of command and control. To do this, we must recognise just how pernicious it is. I've already mentioned the fish being the last to discover water – neuroscience has something to say about this too.

Chapter 8 explored the very different worldviews offered by the left and right brain. It concluded with three thoughts:

- To survive and thrive we need the left and right brain to work together in a complex dance.
- Organisations are becoming increasingly dominated by a left-brain worldview.
- We need to actively correct this imbalance if we are to succeed in projects and in life.

I remind you of this, to encourage you to notice where the left-brain preferences of command and control are woven into the systems and the structures of your projects and organisations. Take orientation to certainty, for example. Are you constrained by a legacy of command and control? Or are you, like the project leaders in the case studies in Chapter 9, seeing the benefits that come when you set up systems and structures to support your project goals?

Viewing projects through a neuroscience lens gives insight into what we experience at a very personal level, and insight into what plays out at a systemic level too.

If we're serious about reducing the number of projects that fail, we need to overturn the legacy of command and control. Yes, there's an art to doing this. However, the vital first step is to choose one of the tools I introduced in Chapters 7 and 8 and give it a go. Talk to colleagues and friends about your experiment and remember – with a Growth Mindset you've nothing to lose!

References

1   Kutsch E, Hall, M, & Turner, N, (2015), *Project Resilience: The Art of Noticing, Interpreting, Preparing, Containing and Recovering*, London: Gower p197

Appendix A: Supporting your professional development

I've written this appendix to answer the question, 'how do the ideas in this book support my professional development?'

I do so by taking a high-level look at the key texts and development frameworks used by three professional bodies: APM (Association for Project Management); PMI (Project Management Institute), and CMI (Change Management Institute).

I make no judgement about which one is better, or which one is most appropriate for you.

If you are not studying for a professional qualification, you may be interested in the question I address in Appendix B: 'How do I apply the ideas in this book to best effect?'

The APM approach

Two key APM texts are designed to support the development of all project professionals, no matter what their level of experience, geography or industry. These are the *APM Body of Knowledge 7th edition* and the *APM Competence Framework*.

APM Body of Knowledge 7th edition

The central idea of the *APM Body of Knowledge 7th edition* is 'the need to balance multiple competing objectives and challenges within a defined set of time, cost and quality constraints in order to achieve beneficial change'.[1]

And that's where the material I've presented in this book comes in – you need to understand 'why people behave as they do', if you are to balance these constraints and achieve beneficial change.

Appendix A: Supporting your professional development

The *APM Body of Knowledge 7th edition* has four chapters:

- Chapter 1, Setting up for success, is primarily for leaders who have to make decisions about how best to use projects, programmes and portfolios (e.g. clients, investing organisations, suppliers, sponsors and SROs).
- Chapter 2, Preparing for change, is primarily for those leading projects, programmes or portfolios of any size and complexity.
- Chapter 3, People and behaviours, is written for anyone involved in projects, programmes and portfolios. Fundamentally, it recognises that success relies on the ability of people to work together.
- Chapter 4, Planning and managing deployment, is for those primarily involved in the end-to-end processes associated with project delivery.

All four deal with the people and processes necessary to deliver projects and change successfully.

While there is an obvious link between the material in this book and the *APM Body of Knowledge 7th edition* Chapters 2 and 3, the advances in neuroscience and tools described throughout these pages are also relevant to Chapters 1 and 4.

Ruth Murray-Webster, editor of the *APM Body of Knowledge 7th edition*, explains. "One of the underlying themes of this book is mindful decision making. It comes up in a slightly different guise in almost every chapter, and it links to Chapter 1 of the *APM Body of Knowledge 7th edition* and the section on strategy in particular. Why are you doing the project in the first place? How does it fit to your strategy? The answers to these questions lead into choices about whether to use projects, programmes or portfolios. And that takes you to questions about how to set up the governance and oversight frameworks to make the big decisions.

"Now, people can do their best. It doesn't matter how hard they work, or how brilliant or personally resilient they are. If they're doing their best in the context of poor decision making, the project is only ever going to go downhill.

"A second theme in this book is leading in uncertainty, and this is highly relevant to the *APM Body of Knowledge 7th edition*, Chapter 4, Planning and managing deployment. The VUCA world means that we need to think hard about appropriate time horizons, and chunking work to make smaller decisions. As things change, it's essential we review what we're doing – properly.

"A big project that was right for today, may not be right six months, or a year, down the line. The world might have changed before you have delivered anything. There's an important question here about psychological safety; do people feel safe enough to say this to the big bosses? Or is it just too dangerous to do so? If it's too dangerous, you'll continue wasting time and effort. The material throughout this book will a) inform your approach to planning and deployment, and b) help you build a psychologically safe environment."

The APM Competence Framework

This framework sets out the competences required for effective project, programme and portfolio management, and for an effective project management office (PMO).

Comprising 29 outcome-based competences, the framework is designed to support individuals, teams and managers as they consider questions such as:

- What should I be able to do in my new role?
- How can I further my career and get to the next stage?
- How can we be sure that we select the right person for the job?
- What can I do to make sure that quality standards are maintained within my team?
- What learning and development do I need to provide for my staff?

Each area in the Framework requires you to consider, when dealing with people, how you get the best out of them. And, just as important, what skills you need to use to help people deliver successfully.

All the material in this book will help you answer these questions. However, when it comes to addressing group and system dynamics, and the challenges and behaviours of stakeholders, customers and team members, some competences carry more significance. Notably,

- Change control
- Conflict resolution
- Contract management
- Governance arrangements
- Leadership
- Requirements management
- Risk and issue management
- Stakeholder engagement and communications management
- Team management

The PMI approach

PMI's approach changed radically with the publication of *A Guide to the Project Management Body of Knowledge, 7th edition* (the *PMBOK® Guide*). The new edition is in two parts: The Standard for Project Management, and A Guide to the Project Management Body of Knowledge. The Standard focuses on value delivery and is principles-based, to guide behaviour. The Guide is focused on performance domains.

The *7th Edition PMBOK® Guide* is shorter and far less prescriptive than earlier editions. This means it is structured around eight outcomes-focused performance domains, rather than the processes and knowledge areas of previous editions.

The Guide introduces the performance domains below. These are broad areas of focus for project delivery and are no longer full of details (inputs, tools and techniques, and outputs). Crucially, they are inter-related, they interact with each other within a project, and they overlap. For example, 'instead of thinking about engaging with the stakeholder in isolation of everything else, you think about the stakeholder, the situation and their impacts across the various project work domains'.[2]

- *Stakeholders*
- *Team*
- Development approach and life cycle
- Planning
- Project work
- Delivery
- Measurement
- *Uncertainty*

There are obvious links between the material in this book and the domains highlighted in italics. Less obvious links with the other domains come to the fore as soon as you read the descriptors and comments.

Take Measurement, for example, Ricardo Vargas explains: "Measurement is all about the *conversations* and *decisions* using the data."[3] As soon as we start speaking about conversations, we're into the material and tools covered in this book. You need to know how to avoid accidentally triggering an avoidance response, for example. Talking about decisions takes us straight to the discussion in this book on cognitive readiness and mindful decision making, and the tools to help you keep your Thinking brain online.

The PMI Standard outlines 12 principles of project management. Once again, these are not prescriptive in nature. They are meant to guide the way project managers – and their teams – can behave to better achieve project outcomes and to deliver lasting value. As with the domains, there are principles (highlighted in italics) with obvious links to the material in this book and, once you get into the detail, many less obvious links to other principles too.

- Be a diligent, respectful, and caring steward
- *Create a collaborative project team environment*
- *Effectively engage with stakeholders*
- Focus on value
- *Recognise, evaluate and respond to system interactions*
- *Demonstrate leadership behaviours*
- Tailor based on context
- Build quality into processes and deliverables
- *Navigate complexity*
- *Optimise risk responses*
- *Embrace adaptability and resiliency*
- *Enable change to achieve the envisioned future state*

The CMI approach

The CMI competence framework sets out 11 key skill topic areas for change managers, and two areas of specialist expertise (see below). These are supported by *CMI's Change Management Body of Knowledge*.

The material in this book speaks to all 11 skill areas, and more so as you move from Foundation level, through Specialist to Master practitioner level. It provides vital building blocks for the skill areas highlighted in *italics*.

- *Facilitating change*
- Impact assessment
- *Strategic thinking*
- *Thinking and judgement*
- *Influencing others*
- *Coaching for change*
- Project management
- *Communicating effectively*

- *Self-management*
- *Facilitation – meetings*
- Professional development
- Training (specialist expertise)
- Communication (specialist expertise)

References

1 Association for Project Management (2019), *APM Body of Knowledge 7th Edition*, page xv
2 Maltzman, R. (2021). *An overview of the 7th Edition PMBOK® Guide*. Boston University. 30 November 2021.
3 Vargas, R. quoted in Maltzman, R. (2021). *An overview of the 7th Edition PMBOK® Guide*. Boston University. 30 November 2021, available at https://get.ricardo-vargas.com/pmbok7canvasen?utm_source=pdf

Appendix B: How do I apply the ideas to best effect?

One of the recurring themes in this book is that *we routinely underestimate what it takes to consolidate learning and change.*

We see this at a team level, a project level and individual level. Given this, it seems important to offer you some thoughts on how to apply the ideas in this book to best effect.

I want to start by drawing your attention to:

- the section on the Growth Mindset, page 39;
- the health warning on page 76. The book contains lots of tools. If you attempt to evaluate them through skim reading, you'll be disappointed with the results. *You have to use them too.*

To get the most from any of the ideas in this book, you'll find it helpful to take your time and mull on them:

- What resonates?
- What's challenging?
- What might it begin to explain?

Remember the construction I introduced on page 121, "I used to ... and now I'm discovering". Try it out for yourself. Go on, I dare you.

My next tip: speak to others about the ideas and the tools, about what you are experimenting with and what you are discovering.

I'm not asking you to be evangelical. I'm encouraging you to be curious.

If talking about this seems a big step, how can you make it safer for yourself? Who do you know, at work or outside of it, that you can talk to? Remember Leonie's story on page 105 – she was very careful in deciding who to speak to about the fog.

Appendix B: How do I apply the ideas in this book to best effect?

Maybe you know others who'd be interested in joining you in a 'thinking' or 'reflection' circle? Or perhaps you are already a member of one?

If you want to experiment with something else, how about sharing one of the case studies in Part 4 with a couple of colleagues?

- What lessons do they take from it?
- What lessons do you take?
- How might you apply these new insights?

And if you're studying for a formal qualification, you could use your studies to frame your reflections, by asking questions like:

- How does this idea/case study stack up with what I am learning about ...?
- What does it add/change/amplify or take away?

That's all I want to say. Now it's over to you.

Appendix C: Putting words on emotions and sensations

Lisa Feldman Barrett explains that the richer our vocabulary, the greater our ability to talk about subtle differences in emotions (emotional granularity).[1] If you have hundreds of words, you have the 'equivalent of a gigantic toolbox fit for a skilled craftsperson'. If you have dozens of words, it's equivalent to 'a run-of-the-mill little red toolbox, filled with some pretty handy tools. Nothing fancy, but they get the job done'. But if you have a limited vocabulary, it's like only having access to 'a hammer and a Swiss Army knife ... a few more tools wouldn't hurt, at least in a Western cultural setting'.

The lists below include around 150 words from Hilary Jacobs Hendel's book, *It's Not Always Depression*.[2] They are intended to help you increase your vocabulary when listening to your body and describing your physical sensations and feelings.

The lists are not exhaustive, and there are overlaps – some words appear in more than one place. Take 'explosive', for example. It is listed with 'angry' and with 'being energised'. There is no right place; the only thing that matters is what the word 'explosive' means to you.

If the lists don't accurately capture what you want to say, try using an image or metaphor, as we did on page 84. It's like ... the sun is rising; a tightly strung tennis racquet; I have to drink from a firehose.

Common words for physical sensations

Angry: fiery, hot, burning, explosive, impulsive;
Tender: cosy, touched, warm, moved, aglow;
Anxiety: queasy, twitchy, pit in stomach, fluttery;
Shame/depressed: empty, frozen, heavy, alone, drained, small, disappearing;
Vulnerable/hurt: bruised, raw, sensitive, wobbly, prickly;
Sad: alone, blue, empty, down, burdened;

Constricted: clenched, blocked, knotted, numb, wooden;
Openhearted: still, spacious, relaxed, alive, flowing, full, expansive;
Scared: sweaty, trembling, cold, shaky, dark;
Energised: bubbly, breathless, fluid, itchy, twitchy, electric, buzzy, alive, explosive;

Words to put language on common emotions

Angry: aggressive, critical, disapproving, frustrated, furious, hostile, jealous, sarcastic, selfish;
Sad: alone, flat, isolated, tired, depressed, ashamed, bored;
Peaceful: accepted, clear, calm, content, relaxed, curious, secure;
Vulnerable/hurt: exposed, humiliated, sensitive, rejected, threatened, avoiding, tight, withdrawn;
Joyful: amused, brave, courageous, excited, playful, wonderful, energetic, joyous;
Ashamed: disrespected, devastated, inferior, ridiculed, insignificant, victimised;
Excited: activated, awed, ecstatic, high, interested, liberated, surprised;
Scared: anxious, fearful, frightened, helpless, overwhelmed, inadequate, terrified, worried, shocked;
Distrustful: astonished, disillusioned, perplexed, suspicious, sceptical;
Confident: amazing, important, creative, strong, powerful, successful, worthwhile, proud;
Guilty: apologetic, avoiding, remorseful;
Disgusted: disapproving, grossed out, rejecting, revolted;
Openhearted: aware, hopeful, inquisitive, tender, thankful, thoughtful, responsive, fulfilled;

References

1 Feldman Barrett, L. (2018), *How Emotions are Made: The Secret Life of the Brain*, London, Pan Books, p106
2 Jacobs Hendel, H. (2018), *It's Not Always Depression*, London, Penguin, p277–283

Acknowledgements

I stand on giants' shoulders.
   My thanks go to:

- All the project managers and leaders I've worked with and learned from, and those who have generously contributed expertise, perspectives and case studies. There are some who I have named in the text and others, whose contribution has been just as important, who have asked to remain anonymous.
- The authors whose work I have referenced, and the Coaches Rising team, who introduced me to several of them through the Neuroscience of Change.
- The team at Coaching through Covid and Beyond – working with you through the early days of the pandemic showed me the power of bringing two very different worldviews together.
- Jo Stanford and Donna Unit for supporting my bid to the APM to publish a text that brings neuroscience to the project world, and to Clare Georgy and James Simons at the APM, for having the courage to accept it.
- Sasi Panchal for her unwavering support, and objective critiques of structure and content.
- Paul Hirst and Rich Maltzman for their contributions to Appendix A.
- The APM reviewers and publications team who have taken my manuscript and turned it into this – a book to be proud of.

And last, but by no means least, to James, my family and friends for their support, encouragement and insights.

We are grateful to the following for permission to reproduce copyright material:

4 Figures from *Project Delivery, Uncertainty and Neuroscience, a Leader's Guide to Walking in Fog* by Carole Osterweil, Visible Dynamics, 2019. Reproduced with permission; The 'SCARF Model' by Dr David Rock, adapted by Cecil in 'Social Neuroscience, SCARF Model and Change Management', https://thehypertextual.com/2013/04/23/social-neuroscience-scarf-model-and-change-management/; An extract from *Stress, Culture and High-Performance Project Teams* by Collin

Acknowledgements

Smith and Carole Osterweil, ICCPM and Visible Dynamics, 2020, https://soundcloud.com/user-680350226/stress_culture_high_performance_project_teams. Reproduced by permission of ICCPM and Carole Osterweil; An extract from *Project Leadership: the game- changer in large scale complex projects*, ICCPM, 2018, https://iccpm.com/project-leadership/. Reproduced by permission of ICCPM; Extracts and figure 1.2 'A survey Measure of Psychological Safety' from *The Fearless Organization: creating psychological safety in the workplace for learning innovation and growth* by Amy C. Edmondson, John Wiley & Sons, 2019, pp.8,20,21,41, copyright © John Wiley & Sons, Inc., 2019. All rights reserved. Permission conveyed through Copyright Clearance Centre; The figure 'The Spiral of Psychological Safety' adapted from Uenlinotes, 2020, https://voynetch.com/4651. Reproduced by kind permission of Chia Uen-Li; An extract from "Emotional Intelligence Domains and Competencies", More Than Sounds LLC, 2017. Reproduced by kind permission of More Than Sounds LLC; A figure and extract from *A Question of Leadership* by Keith Leslie, Bloomsbury Business, an imprint of Bloomsbury Publishing Plc, copyright © Keith Leslie, 2001. Reproduced by permission; Extracts from "How do you manage an invisible workforce?" by Carole Osterweil, *IT NOW*, Vol 63, Issue 1, Spring 2021, Oxford University Press, pp.50-51. Reproduced with permission; Extracts from "Mindful, Getting Started with Mindfulness", Mindful Communications, https://www.mindful.org/meditation/mindfulness-getting-started/. Reproduced with permission; The definition of 'Meditation' from *Cambridge Advanced Learner's Dictionary & Thesaurus*, Cambridge University Press, https://dictionary.cambridge.org/dictionary/english/meditation; Figure 6.4 'The Triple Strand of Influences' from *Understanding and Managing Risk Attitude* by Ruth Murray-Webster and David Hillson, Routledge, 2007, p.93; adapted as Figure 2.1 in *The Disruption Game Plan: New rules for connected thinking on innovation and risk* by Ruth Murray-Webster and Eleanor Winton, Practical Inspiration Publishing. Original reproduced by permission of Taylor and Francis Group, LLC, a division of Informa plc, and adapted version reproduced by permission of Alison Jones Business Services Limited t/a Practical Inspiration Publishing through PLSclear; The figure 'The Cognitive Readiness Framework' from *Cognitive Readiness in Project Teams* by Carl Belack, D. de Filippo, I. de Filippo, Routledge, 2019, Figure 2.1, p.27, copyright © Carl Belack, D. de Filippo, I. de Filippo, 2019. Reproduced by permission of Taylor and Francis Group, LLC, a division of Informa plc; Extracts from *Project Resilience: The Art of Noticing, Interpreting, Preparing, Containing and Recovering* by Elmar Kutsch, Mark Hall and Neil Turner, Routledge, 2015, pp7-10, 197, copyright © Elmar Kutsch, Mark Hall and Neil Turner, 2015.

Reproduced by permission of Taylor and Francis Group, LLC, a division of Informa plc; An extract after "4 Steps to Labeling Emotions for Project Managers" by Ruth Pearce, NPPQ, PMP ACC, Founder ALLE LLC, https://projectmotivator. com/labeling-emotions-lessons-learned-from-in-it-together-group-coaching/. Reproduced by kind permission of the author; The figure 'The four PSI domains', Fearless Organisation Scan. Reproduced with permission; A figure from *Evolving Project Leadership* by Gordon MacKay, APM, p83. Reproduced with kind permission of the author; The figure '10 principles for well-crafted outcome statements' by Alexandra Chapman, Totally Optimized Projects, https://www. totallyoptimizedprojects.com. Reproduced with permission; An extract adapted from "Running the UK's vaccination taskforce" by Nick Elliott, *Project Magazine*, Summer 2021, p39-41. Reproduced by kind permission of the author; An extract from *It's not always depression* by Hilary Jacobs Hendel, Penguin Life, 2018, pp.277-283, copyright © Change triangle LLC, 2018. Reproduced with kind permission of the author and Penguin Books Ltd; And an extract adapted from "Identify dynamics of effective teams", https://rework.withgoogle.com/guides/ understanding-team-effectiveness/steps/identify-dynamics-of-effective-teams/, copyright © Google.

About the author

Carole Osterweil is a project troubleshooter and coach who's on a mission – to bring an understanding of how the human brain works to the world of project management and business transformation.

Carole's pioneering approach is informed by over 20 years as an educator and consultant at Ashridge – Hult business school; her experience as an international project leader endeavoring to Walk in Fog, and her training in psychotherapy and the arts. Now based at Visible Dynamics, she also coaches on the UK Government's Project Leadership Programme at Cranfield University.

Index

Index

Index